U.S. Productivity Growth
Who Benefited?

Research in
Business Economics and
Public Policy, No. 3

Fred Bateman, Series Editor

Chairman and Professor
Business Economics and Public Policy
Indiana University

Other Titles in This Series

No. 1   *The Effectiveness of Antitrust Policy towards Horizontal Mergers*   David B. Audretsch

No. 2   *Organization: The Effect on Large Corporations*   Barry C. Harris

No. 4   *The Changing Structure of Comparative Advantage in American Manufacturing*   Keith E. Maskus

No. 5   *The Dominant Firm: A Study of Market Power* Alice Patricia White

No. 6   *Trends in the Relocation of U.S. Manufacturing*   Christina M.L. Kelton

No. 7   *Inventory and Production Decisions*   Mansfield W. Williams

U.S. Productivity Growth
Who Benefited?

by
Lawrence P. Brunner

UMI RESEARCH PRESS
Ann Arbor, Michigan

Produced and distributed by
UMI Research Press
an imprint of
University Microfilms International
Ann Arbor, Michigan 48106

Library of Congress Cataloging in Publication Data

Brunner, Lawrence P. (Lawrence Philip)
  U.S. productivity growth.

  (Research in business economics and public policy ;
no. 3)
  Revision of the author's thesis—Johns Hopkins
University, 1981.
  Bibliography: p.
  Includes index.
  1. Industrial productivity—United States. 2. Pro-
ductivity accounting. 3. Income distribution—United
States. 4. United States—Economic conditions—
1945-   . I. Title. II. Title: US productivity growth.
III. Title: United States productivity growth. IV. Series.

HC110.I52B78 1983   338'.06'0973   83-9108
ISBN 0-8357-1442-X

Contents

List of Tables   *vii*

Acknowledgments   *xi*

1   Introduction, Model, and Algorithm   *1*
      Introduction   *1*
      The Scarf Algorithm and Its Use   *5*
      Why use this Algorithm?   *5*
      Mechanics of the Algorithm   *7*
      The Model Summarized and Analyzed   *8*
      Consumers   *8*
      Producers   *11*
      Labor Input Types   *15*
      Parameterization in the Scarf Algorithm: Production   *16*
      The Stylized Facts of Growth and Our Model   *23*
      Demand Function Parameterization in the Scarf
      Algorithm   *24*

2   Data Manipulations   *31*
      Introduction   *31*
      Control Totals: Proprietors' Income, Taxes,
      and Savings   *32*
      Reconciliation with National Income and Product
      Accounts   *36*
      Labor and Capital Returns by Industry   *39*
      Capital Input Data   *41*
      Labor Input Data   *45*
      Industry Interrelationships: Input-Output, Final Demand, and
      Personal Consumption Expenditure by Industry   *49*
      Input-Output Data   *49*
      Definition of Structures and Equipment Industries   *53*
      Personal Consumption Expenditures   *54*

3   Simulation Results   *57*
     Simulations and Reasons for Performance of Different
     Runs   *57*
     Zero Productivity Change Simulation Effects   *61*
     Zero Productivity Change in Particular Industries   *76*
     Alternative Assumptions on Overall Productivity
     Growth   *89*
     Predicting with Our Model   *96*
     Conclusion   *100*

4   Induced Accumulation and Productivity Change   *103*
     Introduction   *103*
     Results   *105*
     Introduction and First Results   *105*
     Comparison with Hulten (1975)   *107*
     Further Results: Long-Run Fisherian Rate of
     Technical Change   *108*
     Effective Rates of Productivity Change: Total Economy   *110*
     Intertemporal Accounting and the Importance of
     Productivity Change   *112*
     Sectoral Effective Rates of Productivity Change   *116*
     Conclusion   *118*

Appendix   *119*

Notes   *123*

Bibliography   *133*

Index   *145*

List of Tables

2.1. Comparison Between Our National Accounting Framework and the NIPA Statistical Tables for 1967   *36*

2.2. Receipt and Expenditure Items Included in the Government Sector, 1967   *38*

2.3. Example of Determination of Total Units of Labor in Our Economy for a Hypothetical Situation   *40*

2.4. Occupational Mobility: Percentage of Workers with a Different One-Digit Occupation in 1970 and 1965   *47*

2.5. Fixed Capital Formation by Industry, 1967 ($mn.)   *53*

2.6. Consumption Table: Classification of Consumption Goods by Types of Product and by Industry Division   *55*

3.1. Comparison of 1974 (End-of-Simulation Period) Values Between Run 2 and the Control Solution   *62*

3.2. Comparison of 1974 Capital Input and Total Output Between Run 2 and Run 1   *64*

3.3. Comparison of 1974 Labor Input Values Between Run 2 and Run 1   *65*

3.4. Average Annual Percentage Growth Rates of Capital and Labor, 1947-74, and Percentage Differences in Growth Rates   *66*

3.5. Average Annual Percentage Growth Rates of Total Input, 1947-74, and Percentage Differences in Growth Rates   *66*

3.6. Average Annual Percentage Growth Rates of Gross Output, Intermediate Input, and Value-Added, 1947-74, and Percentage Differences in Growth Rates   *67*

3.7. Comparison of 1974 Gross Output, Intermediate Input, and Value-Added by Industry Between Run 2 and Run 1   *68*

3.8.   Average Annual Percentage Growth Rates of Producer Prices and Productivity, 1947-74   *69*

3.9.   End-of-Period Percentage Differences in Consumption Goods by Type of Product Between Run 2 and Run 1   *69*

3.10.   Average Annual Percentage Growth Rates in Capital and Labor Prices, 1947-74, and Percentage Differences in Growth Rates   *71*

3.11.   Average Annual Percentage Growth Rates of Aggregate Input Prices, 1947-74, and Percentage Differences in Growth Rates   *71*

3.12.   Comparison of 1974 Input Prices by Input Type Between Run 2 and Run 1   *72*

3.13.   Differences in Average Annual Percentage Growth Rates of Prices and Quantities of Value-Added and Aggregate Input, 1947-74   *72*

3.14.   Comparison of 1974 Factor Shares by Input Type Between Run 2 and Run 1   *75*

3.15.   Comparison of 1974 Overall Capital and Labor Shares by Industry Between Run 2 and Run 1   *75*

3.16.   Comparison of 1974 Capital-Labor Ratios in Production Between Runs 3-7 and Run 1   *76*

3.17.   Output Shares and Capital-Labor Ratios by Industry, Runs 1 and 7   *77*

3.18.   Comparison of 1974 Capital Inputs by Industry Between Runs 3-7 and Run 1   *79*

3.19.   Comparison of 1974 Labor Inputs by Industry Between Runs 3-7 and Run 1   *79*

3.20.   Comparison of 1974 Total Input by Industry Between Runs 3-7 and Run 1   *80*

3.21.   Comparison of 1974 Output-Labor Ratios Between Runs 3-7 and Run 1   *80*

3.22.   Average Annual Percentage Growth Rates of Gross Output, 1947-74, for Runs 3-7 and Run 1 by Industry   *81*

3.23.   Average Annual Percentage Growth Rates of Intermediate Input, 1947-74, for Runs 3-7 and Run 1 by Industry   *81*

3.24.   Average Annual Percentage Growth Rates of Value-Added, 1947-74, for Runs 3-7 and Run 1 by Industry   *82*

3.25. Percentage Differences in Average Annual Growth Rates of Gross Output Between Runs 3-7 and Run 1 by Industry   *82*

3.26. Percentage Differences in Average Annual Growth Rates of Intermediate Input Between Runs 3-7 and Run 1   *83*

3.27. Percentage Differences in Average Annual Growth Rates of Value-Added Between Runs 3-7 and Run 1   *83*

3.28. Comparison of 1974 Producer Goods Prices by Industry Between Runs 3-7 and Run 1   *84*

3.29. Percentage Differences in Average Annual Growth Rates of Capital Input Price Between Runs 3-7 and Run 1 by Industry   *85*

3.30. Percentage Differences in Average Annual Growth Rates of Labor Input Price Between Runs 3-7 and Run 1 by Industry   *85*

3.31. Percentage Differences in Average Annual Growth Rates of Aggregate Input Price Between Runs 3-7 and Run 1 by Industry   *86*

3.32. Comparison of 1974 Values of Input Prices by Type of Input Between Runs 3-7 and Run 1   *86*

3.33. Comparison of 1974 Factor Shares by Input Type Between Runs 3-7 and Run 1 for the Total Economy   *87*

3.34. Comparison of 1974 Capital Shares by Industry Between Runs 3-7 and Run 1   *88*

3.35. Comparison of 1974 Labor Shares by Industry Between Runs 3-7 and Run 1   *88*

3.36. Comparison of 1974 Capital-Labor Ratios by Industry Between Runs 8-11 and Run 1   *90*

3.37. Comparison of 1974 Output-Labor Ratios by Industry Between Runs 8-11 and Run 1   *90*

3.38. Comparison of 1974 Capital Input Overall and by Industry Between Runs 8-11 and Run 1   *91*

3.39. Comparison of 1974 Labor Input by Industry Between Runs 8-11 and Run 1   *91*

3.40. Comparison of 1974 Total Input by Industry Between Runs 8-11 and Run 1   *92*

3.41. Average Annual Percentage Changes in Total Factor Productivity (Value-Added Base), and Differences from Actual Growth   *92*

3.42. Average Annual Growth Rates of Gross Output, Intermediate Input, and Value-Added for Runs 8-11, and Differences from Run 1   *94*

3.43. Comparison of 1974 Producer and Consumer Prices by Industry Between Runs 8-11 and Run 1   *95*

3.44. Average Annual Growth Rates of Prices of Capital by Industry and Differences Between Runs 8-11 and Run 1   *95*

3.45. Average Annual Growth Rates of Prices of Labor by Industry and Differences Between Runs 8-11 and Run 1   *96*

3.46. Average Annual Growth Rates of Total Input Price by Industry and Differences Between Runs 8-11 and Run 1   *96*

3.47. Percentage Changes in End-of-Period Input Price and Factor Shares by Type of Input (Runs 8-11/Run 1)   *97*

3.48. Percentage Change in End-of-Period Capital and Labor Shares by Industry (Runs 8-11/Run 1)   *97*

3.49. Percentage Differences in Aggregate Economy Variables (Simulated/Actual)   *99*

3.50. Percentage Differences in Consumption Goods by Type of Product (Simulated/Actual)   *99*

4.1. Sources of Growth of Real Product, 1947-74 (Average Annual Percentage Growth Rates)   *106*

4.2. Sources of Growth of Real Product, 1948-66 (Average Annual Percentage Growth Rates Computed using Christensen-Jorgenson Data)   *108*

4.3. Sources of Growth of Real Product, 1948-66 (Average Annual Percentage Growth Rates Computed Using Our Data)   *108*

4.4. Average Annual Growth Rates, 1947-74   *110*

4.5. Average Annual Growth Rates of Productivity: Sectoral Effective and Actual Rates, 1947-74   *111*

4.6. Average Annual Growth Rates of Productivity, Output, and Contribution of Productivity Growth to Output Growth   *116*

4.7. Computation of Overall Effective Rates of Productivity Change   *117*

Acknowledgments

I am deeply grateful to both Dr. Charles R. Hulten and Dr. Hugh Rose. My debt to them is enormous and is more than can be expressed in a few lines. Dr. Hulten has guided my work ever since I first became interested in the topic of productivity. His perceptive comments have been instrumental in giving my work whatever merit it possesses. Dr. Rose has given me the benefit of his vast experience and his comments on my work have significantly improved it in many areas. The help of these two has made a tremendous impact on my professional life and on this study.

I am indebted to Dr. J. Randolph Norsworthy, of the Office of Productivity and Technology, U.S. Bureau of Labor Statistics, who saw enough promise in my work to extend support to me for a year to enable my work to proceed. His help and that of his colleagues in the Office of Productivity has been instrumental in enabling me to complete this work. I would especially like to thank Bob Bechtold of BLS for his cheerful help with my computer problems, without which I might still be computing. Also, I wish to acknowledge the help of Leo Sveikauskas and Michael Harper of BLS for their help and encouragement.

I wish to thank Dr. A. Thomas King, from whom I obtained a copy of the Scarf algorithm suitable for use on a computer, and also Dr. Don Fullerton, whose help enabled me to overcome computational problems with the algorithm. In addition, to all of my former teachers and friends at Johns Hopkins University, especially Dr. Louis Maccini and Dr. Bob Rossana, I am grateful for encouragement and for providing an atmosphere of friendship and intellectual curiosity.

I want to express my appreciation to my wife, Marty, for her patience and help while I completed my seemingly endless work. Without her support, it would not have been possible. I also wish to thank my parents, especially for their help during my first year.

This volume is dedicated to my family.

1

Introduction, Model, and Algorithm

Introduction

In an important paper, Robert Solow (1958) stimulated work in the productivity field. He showed that there was an economic justification for the use of the "residual," which is the growth rate of real output that is not explained by an index of the growth rates of real inputs.[1] If we assume a linear homogeneous aggregate production function, that factors of production are paid their marginal products, and also that productivity change can be represented by the rise in a factor which multiplies the efficiency of both inputs by the same amount (Hicks-neutrality), then the conventional residual is equivalent to the growth rate of the Hicksian efficiency parameter. Mathematically, we have:

(1.1) $\text{Residual} = \dot{A}/A = \dot{Q}/Q - M_K(\dot{K}/K) - M_L(\dot{L}/L)$

where Q is value added, K is capital input, L is labor input, M_K and M_L are factor shares,

(1.2) $Q = A F(K,L)$

where F is a a linear homogeneous production function.[2] In the more general case of factor augmentation, the residual will still measure technical change, but it cannot be identified with a single parameter.

The great advantage of the residual method for finding productivity growth rates (total factor productivity change) is that the Hicksian parameter (A) can be measured using only empirically available prices and quantities. From this method, we may derive an estimate of the rate at which the production function (1.2) is shifting over time. Thus the residual is a valid measure of the shift in technology under our assumptions.

In addition, we can use the residual to answer the question: What percentage of output growth is due to productivity change? Normally, the answers to this question were obtained by dividing the residual by output growth, or in other words: $(\dot{A}/A)/(\dot{Q}/Q)$. For example, Solow found that 87.5% of the increase in output per man-hour was attributable to technical change.[3]

However, in the analysis of productivity and economic growth we are often interested in a different question, which is: What is the total contribution of productivity change to economic growth? Put another way, if $\dot{A}/A$ was zero, what would $\dot{Q}/Q$ have been? We know that the capital input which we observe historically is endogenous. A rise in total factor productivity will, in general, lead to a rise in output, and then to more saving and capital formation. Because of the endogeneity of the capital stock, if productivity change had occurred at a different rate the growth rate of capital would have been different. But when we use the number $[\dot{A}/A]/[\dot{Q}/Q]$ to measure the contribution of productivity change to growth, we are assuming through our computation of the residual that capital stock growth would have been the same if productivity had grown at a different rate. Thus a conceptual distinction arises between two different questions:

(A)   What has been the rise in productive efficiency for given inputs of capital and labor?

(B)   What has been the *total* contribution of productivity change to the growth process?

The answers to these questions are only the same if capital stock is unaffected by the growth process, which is untrue. (We are assuming throughout that labor input growth can be taken as being exogenous.)

We will define K^* as the capital stock which would have existed in the absence of productivity change. Since capital stock growth is an increasing function of productivity growth, we have:

(1.3) $\dot{K}/K = \dot{K}^*/K^*.$

The difference between K and K^* represents the difference between the total contribution of productivity change to growth and the rate at which the production function is shifting over time.

Let us now rewrite our residual (1.1) as:

(1.1') $\dot{A}/A = \dot{Q}/Q - M_L(\dot{L}/L) - M_K[\dot{K}/K - \dot{K}^*/K^* + \dot{K}^*/K^*]$

or:

(1.1'') $\dot{A}/A + M_K[\dot{K}/K - \dot{K}^*/K^*] = \dot{Q}/Q - M_L(\dot{L}/L) - M_K(\dot{K}^*/K^*).$

Our measure of the total effect of productivity change on growth is then:[4]

(1.4) $\quad Z = \dot{A}/A + M_K[\dot{K}/K - \dot{K}^*/K^*] > \dot{A}/A$

because $\dot{K}/K$ is greater than $\dot{K}^*/K^*$. The presumption is thus that the dynamic residual Z is larger than the normal residual, so that productivity change measured this way is responsible for a much larger fraction of growth than the conventional measures would lead one to believe.[5]

To show the effects of productivity changes on the economy more clearly, let us consider an economy with one productive sector, constant tastes and technology, and investment equal to replacement.[6] The production function is represented by curve Oac in figure 1.1. Given initial K_{t0} and L_{t0}, the economy is at point a at time $t0$. Now assume a one time only rise in productivity that is Hicks neutral. The production function shifts upward to curve Ob. Output will then increase, some of the extra output will be saved and invested, and the capital stock will rise, until new investment is in line with replacement of old capital at time $t1$. In this case, we can measure the rise in output bd, and split it into its components: the rise in efficiency for a given level of input (bc or af), and the rise in output from the induced capital accumulation (cd).

Figure 1.1

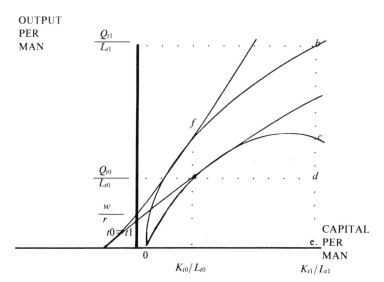

Note: A similar version of this diagram is found in Hulten (1975). We assume here that $L_{t0} = L_{t1}$. The two curves are drawn so that technical progress is Hicks-neutral. However, this form of technical progress is not necessary for the effects that we are discussing to occur.

Under our assumptions of a linear homogeneous production function with Hicks-neutral technical change, and assuming factors are paid their marginal products, the conventional total factor productivity index A_{t1}/A_{t0} is a measure of the ratio be/ce.[7]

Without the rise in efficiency, output per man would be still at the initial level, as would capital per man. In this case, all the increased capital was induced by productivity change since this was assumed to be the only change between $t0$ and $t1$. Thus $\dot{K}^*$ equals zero, which is less than $\dot{K}$. In this framework, the total importance of technical change is measured by the ratio be/de. It is this ratio which this work attempts to measure and analyze.

There have been previous attempts to account for the endogeneity or reproducibility of capital and its effects on productivity.[8] Our approach resembles that of Hulten.[9] We begin with data on U.S. real output, labor, capital, and intermediate input, which has been assembled and conforms to U.S. national income and product account definitions for the years 1947-74.[10] We then use this model to specify production and consumption functions for the U.S. economy using a highly aggregated dynamic model for this period. In addition, the government and foreign sectors are treated, and interindustry transactions are included in the model. We use this model to simulate the U.S. economy's growth path under varying assumptions on the growth rates of total factor productivity. To check the model's accuracy, a control run is performed which replicates the actual performance of the U.S. economy over the sample period quite closely. We can then vary the rates of productivity change and determine the effects of such variation on overall capital accumulation, on the functional distribution of income, on the real output in particular sectors, and on real consumption expenditure and consumer utility. Thus the question of the overall importance of productivity change for growth can be answered in an appropriate framework, along with other questions.

Using data from Jorgenson and Christensen, Hulten shows that for the U.S. in the period 1948-66 the conventional residual accounted for 34% of output growth, while the dynamic residual (Z) explains 64% of growth when the capital accumulation *induced* by output growth is taken into account. In a later work, Hulten (1979) confirms this result by developing an intertemporal accounting framework. He is able to show that his intertemporal residual is identical with the changes in Malinvaud's intertemporal production possibility frontier. In this model, 66% of output growth is due to total factor productivity change. Hulten also uses his framework to derive and generalize Domar's aggregation results. These results serve both as a justification for use of the conventional residual, and as an extension of the conventional growth accounting analysis.

One major question which this framework enables us to answer is the effect of technical change on the distribution of income between labor and capital and between different occupational groups of labor. Who has benefited the most from technical change? Alternatively, what is the incidence of productivity change? Our model is able to answer these questions by examining the historical functional distribution between structures, equipment, white-collar workers, skilled blue-collar workers, and unskilled workers. By varying rates of total factor productivity change, and especially by holding the growth rates of the Hicksian efficiency parameters to zero for all sectors, we can examine the changes in factor shares induced by productivity changes. As a first approximation, we would expect to find that white-collar workers were helped by productivity change relative to unskilled blue-collar workers because productivity change should have raised the demand for white-collar workers. This is especially true since labor in the agricultural sector was predominantly unskilled at the beginning of the period under study, and agricultural productivity change led to massive reductions in the numbers of workers in agriculture, and their transfer to other employment.

In addition, we have a model which can take into account intertemporal consumption decisions and the growth of the capital stock over time. We are interested in determining the time path of K^* in (1.4) given alternative assumptions on productivity change. For example, if we want to see the effects of U.S. manufacturing sector productivity growth between 1947 and 1974, simulating the model with no productivity growth in manufacturing over this period and comparing the growth rate of capital over the period with our control solution (based on actual data) gives us an estimate of K^* and K. This then enables us to compute the dynamic residual Z, giving us the true impact of technical change on growth.[11]

Before proceeding further, we should clarify the implications of one assumption we have made. In our work, technical progress is assumed to be "disembodied." In other words, technical change occurs as if floating down from heaven, like the proverbial manna, and changes in the rate of investment do not affect the rate of technical progress. There has been some theoretical work criticizing this assumption [see Solow (1959), Arrow (1962), Kaldor and Mirrlees (1962)]. Empirical work on the subject has had mixed results, with Intriligator (1965) obtaining results supporting embodiment, while Wickens (1970), You (1976), Gregory and James (1973), and Barger (1976) finding evidence against it. Theoretical criticisms of embodiment have been made by Jorgenson (1966) and Denison (1964). In view of the lack of evidence for the superiority of an alternative assumption, we will use the disembodied specification of technical change.

The Scarf Algorithm and Its Use

Why use this Algorithm?

The techniques which we will use in this analysis are general equilibrium techniques. They are generalizations and modifications of techniques originally developed for the analysis of tax incidence and international trade. It will be recognized that general equilibrium methods are designed for the determination of relative price changes. Thus we do not determine the absolute price level or the inflation rate in our model.

One of the first and most important of the applications of the Scarf algorithm was Shoven and Whalley's work (1972). They applied the algorithm to the problem of determining the incidence of the corporate income tax. Shoven and Whalley were able to extend the analysis of Herberger (1962) in this area (see also chapter 2). The Scarf algorithm enabled them to examine the effects of a labor-leisure choice, the effects of many distortions rather than just one, and to simultaneously compute the incidence and efficiency effects of changes in government policy, none of which was possible before. In addition, models with many goods and factors can be conveniently dealt with. Thus the use of computable general equilibrium techniques enables substantial advances to be made.

Although much of the analysis using the Scarf algorithm has focused on tax problems, we plan to use it in another context. In this work, we will examine the incidence of productivity change on the functional distribution of income, in addition to other topics. Because we are examining this question, we are employing tools that have been used previously in incidence analysis. Although use of the Scarf algorithm frees us from many restrictions, there are some aspects of an actual economy which we are unable to deal with in this paper.

The business cycle, inflation, and unemployment are all issues which we do not choose to include in this analysis. In this we follow the literature on tax incidence and previous work with the algorithm. The macroeconomic effects of productivity change are thus not included in our analysis. Since tax incidence deals primarily with changes in relative prices and not absolute prices, we feel justified in excluding business cycle effects. We are compensated for the consequent loss of realism by a gain in simplicity and tractability. In addition, we do not confuse effects due to government stabilization policy with those due to the productivity changes we are trying to analyze. We believe that we can generate useful results with our model, although we do run into what George F. Break calls "the basic dilemma of incidence analysis: the need to deal with all the complex interrelationships of modern economic systems, and the practical impossibility of doing so."[12]

We can think of the results of our model in the following way. We are assuming that the economy is in a long run equilibrium in all years. If it actually is not and we have booms, depressions, and other short run disequilibria, then we can think of the fluctuations as cancelling each other out so that, on the average, we are in a situation of equilibrium. The model then is simulating a trend rate of growth which the actual economy fluctuates around. We then pretend that the short run disequilibria can be modelled by assuming that labor and capital stocks fall during a short run disequilibrium.

Mechanics of the Algorithm

The Scarf algorithm is a computational method, derived from combinatorial topology, which can find an approximate fixed point (an approximate solution) for a general nonlinear system of equations. The development of the algorithm was important, since "prior to the last several years no procedure had ever been suggested that could determine the solution of a general Walrasian model of even modest size with a reasonable amount of computing time."[13]

Due to the fact that the algorithm's mechanics are discussed elsewhere [see Scarf (1973)], we will restrict ourselves here to an overview of the algorithm's properties. The Scarf algorithm determines an equilibrium price vector for a competitive economy. This price vector is composed of prices of all outputs and inputs, although in certain cases the dimensionality of the problem may be reduced or increased. The equilibrium price vector computed has the property that productive techniques which are employed have profits equal to zero at those prices, and productive techniques not used have profits less than or equal to zero.[14]

Some assumptions are required in order to make use of the algorithm. First, the market demand functions must satisfy Walras' law (this will occur if they are derived from utility functions, as ours are). Second, constant returns to scale in production (linear homogeneity) must be assumed.

Productive techniques can be represented for purposes of computation by either production functions, or fixed coefficient activity vectors, whichever is desired. Consumer incomes depend on the market prices of their endowments, and also on their shares of government revenue which is redistributed to them. Governments can redistribute income in this model, collect taxes, and also act as consumers themselves.

Given a starting point, the algorithm proceeds until a solution is found, giving us an approximation to a competitive equilibrium for any specified degree of accuracy. A crude approximation is first found, and then the approximation is refined. It has been shown that the algorithm cannot cycle, and will converge in finite time. In addition, existence of general equilibrium in models of this sort has been shown by Scarf (1967, 1973) in the absence of taxes, and by Shoven (1973, 1974) and Shoven and Whalley (1973) in the presence of taxes. Without these existence proofs, it would be hard to imagine computing meaningful equilibria under various tax regimes. The uniqueness of equilibrium has not been shown but, in practice, multiple equilibria have not been a problem.

Scarf notes that the algorithm "derives its importance from the observation that for most problems it will terminate in a far smaller number of iterations than the theoretical upper bound..."[15] This is one advantage. Another is the fact that use of the algorithm avoids the restrictiveness of previous general equilibrium models. Many types of goods, factors of production, and different kinds of consumers can be modelled, and many distortions in the economy (taxes, monopoly, unionization, etc.) can be handled at the same time. In addition, because the model is not a local approximation [unlike the Harberger (1962) model] large changes in the magnitudes of taxes and other distortions can be handled easily.

Models which can be solved by using the algorithm have been applied to problems in tax incidence, international trade problems, urban economics, and welfare economics [see King (1977, 1980), Miller and Spencer (1977), Arnott and MacKinnon (1977)]. It has been shown that the use of general equilibrium techniques greatly improves the results obtainable on the efficiency losses of taxation [Whalley (1975)].

The Model Summarized and Analyzed

The properties of the model which we will use to analyze productivity will be discussed in the following section. The assumptions about consumers, producers, saving behavior, and input types will be delineated and examined.

Consumers

We will assume that all consumers are alike. Thus each consumer will be endowed with the average capital and labor endowment of the economy. This is a large simplification, but it serves to focus on the functional distributions of income, which is the main interest of this paper.

Consumer behavior in our model will be described by a utility function of the linear expenditure system (LES) form. In (1.5) through (1.10), C represents aggregate consumption, S is aggregate gross private saving (the sum of net personal saving, net corporate saving, and capital consumption allowances), U is a utility function, C_i represents individual consumption goods, and α, β_i, and m_i are parameters:

$$(1.5) \qquad U(C) = \left[\sum_{i=1}^{9} (C_i - m_i)^{\beta_i}\right]^{\alpha} S^{(1-a)} \quad ; \quad \sum_{i=1}^{9} \beta_i = 1$$

By taking logs, we have:

$$(1.6) \qquad \text{Log}[U(C)] = \alpha \left[\sum_{i=1}^{9} \beta_i (C_i - m_i)\right] + (1-\alpha)S; \quad \sum_{i=1}^{9} \beta_i = 1$$

Maximization of (1.5) or (1.6) subject to a budget constraint (with $[C_i - m_i]$ as a variable, not C_i):

(1.7) $\quad \sum_{i=1}^{9} \quad p_i C_i + p_s S = Y$

leads to the linear expenditure system for demands:[16]

(1.8) $\quad p_i C_i = p_i m_i + \quad \alpha \beta_i [Y - \sum p_i m_i], \qquad\qquad i = 1, \ldots, 9$

$\qquad p_s S = (1 - \alpha)[Y - \sum p_i m_i].$

There is a simple interpretation of the parameters. If they are positive, the elements m_i represent necessary consumption, or those quantities of goods which the consumer buys first. The consumer's residual or "supernumary" consumption is then spent in fixed proportions β_i between all the consumption goods. If the m_i are negative, there is no supernumary consumption of that particular good.

The income elasticities $\xi(C_i)$, own price elasticities $\xi(C_i, C_i)$, and cross-price elasticities $\xi(C_i, C_j)$ are computed as follows:

(1.9) $\quad \xi(C_i) \quad = \beta_i Y / (p_i C_i)$

$\qquad \xi(C_i, C_i) = -1 + (1 - \beta_i) m_i / C_i$

$\qquad \xi(C_i, C_j) = -\beta_i p_j m_j / (p_i C_i)$

We can see from these formulas that inferior goods are impossible in this model, and that all goods which are price elastic have m_i parameters less than zero.

The utility function (1.5 or 1.6) is additive and exhibits strong separability between all pairs of goods. Strotz (1957) and Gorman (1959) point out that if we consider each of the C_i's to be an aggregate of many individual goods that we are assuming the consumer first decides how much expenditure to allocate to each of the aggregates consumption and savings, and then allocates his consumption expenditure among the individual consumption goods in each group. The model is known as a utility tree. However, due to limitations on computing time, and in order to reduce the size of the model, we will consider only ten aggregate consumption goods: food, clothing, personal care, housing, household operation, medical care, personal business, transportation, other consumption, and savings.

Deaton (1974) has criticized the assumption of additivity as implying extremely strong restrictions on the price and income elasticities.[17] We have chosen, however, to keep the assumption for two reasons. First, the model's parameters can be easily chosen, and the demand functions are computationally simple. In a model with this many parameters, ease of computation is essential. Second, alternative models which reject the additivity assumption (loglinear and Rotterdam models) are unsatisfactory on theoretical grounds, since they "are both fundamentally inconsistent with utility maximization."[18] We therefore cannot use them, since we need demand functions which satisfy Walras' law, which they will if derived from utility functions.

The demand functions we use will be homogeneous of zero degree in all prices. This property is necessary to enable use of the price normalization that the prices sum to unity, because the algorithm works on the unit simplex. As long as the demand functions are derived by maximizing utility subject to a budget constraint and there are no progressive income taxes, we have no problem. Progressive income taxes can be modelled by assuming several groups of consumers, from poor to rich, and giving each group a constant marginal tax rate which increases as we move up the income scale from one group to another, although we do not do this.

Savings rate. One final assumption will be made in this model relating to consumers. We will assume a constant gross private savings rate. In other words, the sum of net personal saving, net corporate saving, and capital consumption allowances will be our measure of private saving, and this will be a constant proportion of our income measure, which also includes these three items (see chapter 3).

There is a good deal of evidence in favor of this assumption in works of Denison (1958), and David and Scadding (1974). David and Scadding note that the gross private saving rate (GPSR) including consumer durables and their imputed return has no trend over the 1898-1969 period, and the year-to-year variation in the GPSR is small except for World War I, World War II, and the Depression. If we do not define saving as including consumer durables, then the GPSR has been constant since World War I, with the same periods (World War II and the Depression) excepted.

The assumption of a constant gross private savings rate has many implications. First, if this is true, the interest elasticity of savings should be zero. Secondly, since gross private savings includes personal and corporate saving, we may treat these two types of saving as perfect substitutes. The empirical work shows that total saving (the corporate plus personal total) is more stable than either of its component parts, and that changes in personal saving tend to be balanced by equal and opposite changes in corporate saving. Third, the rise in the share of output absorbed by the public sector has had no effect on private saving.

Finally, if all this is true, it implies that households are "ultrarational," or that in other words they treat corporations as extensions of themselves. This may not be quite as farfetched as it appears at first. David and Scadding note that tax changes have tended to subsidize corporate saving relative to individual saving, and since both stockholders and the largest savers tend to be in high income brackets, tax changes affecting them tend to have important effects. As we note in the discussion of the data, in our general equilibrium model, we must specify some means through which the consumers own the assets of the economy.[19] If consumers own the economy's assets then treating their personal saving and corporate savings as identical, as we do in this model, is not farfetched. The empirical evidence suggests that doing so gives a reasonable representation of the actual situation.[20]

This assumption implies certain things about the utility function. Given our utility function (1.5 or 1.6), we derive

$$(1.10) \quad p_s S = (1 - \alpha)[Y - \sum_{i=1}^{n} p_i m_i]$$

which implies that the savings rate $p_s S / Y$ is not constant unless the $(p_i m_i)$ terms sum to zero. Thus this will be assumed in the empirical work.

We note that in our model aggregate saving (S) will be invested without any Keynesian difficulties of intended investment not being equal to savings. Since we will employ two types of capital goods in this model (structures and equipment), the allocation of investment funds between the different types of capital becomes a problem. This problem is dealt with later in this chapter.

Producers

We are assuming that production possibilities may be represented by the linearly homogeneous constant elasticity of substitution (CES) production functions. There will be constant elasticities of substitution between labor and capital in the production of value-added, along with fixed coefficients between intermediate input and gross output (which is the sum of value-added and intermediate input). More formally, we can write:

$$(1.11) \quad O_i = A_i \left[a_i K_i^{(s-1)/s} + (1 - a_i) L_i^{(s-1)/s} \right]^{s/(s-1)} + \sum_{j=1}^{6} V_{ij}$$

$$O_i = Q_i + \sum_{j=1}^{6} V_{ij} \quad ; \quad i,j = 1, \ldots, 6.$$

where:

O_i = gross output in industry i

Q_i = value-added in industry i

V_{ij} = intermediate input from industry i to industry j

K_i, L_i = aggregate capital and labor input in industry i, defined in (1.33) and (1.34).

s = elasticity of substitution between capital and labor

A_i = Hicksian productivity parameter

a_i = capital-labor distribution parameter.

Also, we have:

(1.12) $\quad V_{ij} = \eta_{ij} O_i \quad i = 1, \ldots, 6 \,; j = 1, \ldots, 6.$

where η_{ij} is a fixed coefficient relating the amount of jth industry output required to produce one unit of output of industry i. By assuming fixed coefficients here, we can quite simply determine producer prices for gross output once we determine value added by industry. This assumption saves much computational time.

We need to account for interindustry sales because they may have a large effect on the residuals which we compute. Domar (1962) and Hulten (1975) show that because industries sell to each other, aggregate rates of productivity growth for the entire economy will be equal to the weighted *sum* (not average) of the individual sectoral gross output residuals, with the weights summing to more than one. Thus the total effect of sectoral productivity change on the overall transformation curve is greater than the direct effects of sectoral productivity change, because of interindustry transactions. In other words, the aggregate rate of productivity change for an economy is T, where:

$$(1.13) \quad T = \sum_{i=1}^{n} \left[\frac{p_i O_i}{\sum_{j=1}^{n} p_j Q_j} \quad (\dot{A}_i / A_i) \right]$$

and where the sum of the weights is greater than one.

The six industries which we use are:

(1) Agriculture

(2) Residual industry—everything nowhere else classified

(3) Structures-producing industry

(4) Manufacturing

(5) Equipment-producing

(6) Services

The definition of industries and derivations of industry data is discussed in chapter 2, on data.

There are two types of capital goods which we employ in this model: structures and equipment. These are defined as discussed in chapter 2. We aggregate these into an overall capital stock using a Cobb-Douglas function:

$$(1.14) \quad K_i = [K_{Si}]^{C_i} [K_{Ei}]^{1 - c_i} \quad ; \quad i = 1, \ldots, 6$$

where the S and E denote structures and equipment. This aggregate capital stock is a fiction (as is overall labor) which we employ for simplicity. Consumers actually own stocks of structures and equipment capital. The chief advantage of this formulation is the simplicity and ease of computation which it gives to the determination of the separate input demands.

We also employ three different types of labor input: white-collar, skilled blue-collar, and unskilled. These are aggregated into an overall labor input in the same manner as capital:

$$(1.15) \quad L_i = [L_{1i}]^{g_{1i}} [L_{2i}]^{g_{2i}} [L_{3i}]^{g_{3i}} \quad ; \quad \sum_{j=1}^{3} g_{ji} = 1.$$

The consumers (who are all alike) are considered to own stocks of each type of labor input.

By substituting (1.14) and (1.15) into the production function (1.11) and maximizing profit, we may determine the demands for structures inputs explicitly:

$$(1.16) \quad K_S = [Q/A] \left[a \left| \frac{r_S(1 - c)}{r_E d} \right|^{(1-c)(s-1)/s} + \left| \frac{r_S}{w_1 X} \right|^{s-1} \right.$$

$$\times \quad (1 - a) \left| \frac{w_1 g_2}{w_2 g_1} \right|^{\frac{g_2(s-1)}{s}} \left| \frac{w_1 g_3}{w_3 g_1} \right|^{\frac{g_3(s-1)}{s}} \left. \right]^{s/(s-1)}$$

where r_S, r_E, w_1, w_2, w_3 represent factor prices of structures, equipment, white-collar labor, skilled blue-collar labor, and unskilled workers, and X is:

$$(1.17) \quad X = \frac{ac}{(1 - a)g_1} \left[\frac{r_S(1 - c)}{r_E c} \right]^{-\frac{(s-1)}{s}} \left[\left| \frac{w_1 g_2}{w_2 g_1} \right|^{g_2} \left| \frac{w_1 g_3}{w_3 g_1 1} \right|^{g_3} \right]^{\frac{(1-s)}{s}}$$

In similar fashion, we may determine the cost-minimizing demand for white-collar workers:

$$(1.18) \quad L_1 = [Q/A] \left[a \left| \frac{r_S(1-c)}{r_{EC}} \right|^{\frac{(1-c)(s-1)}{s}} \left| \frac{w_1 X}{r_S} \right|^{(s-1)} + (1-a) \right.$$

$$\left. \times \left| \frac{w_1 g_2}{w_2 g_1} \right|^{\frac{g_2(s-1)}{s}} \left| \frac{w_1 g_3}{w_3 g_1} \right|^{\frac{g_3(s-1)}{s}} \right]^{s/(1-s)} .$$

The demands for equipment and the other two types of labor follow a similar pattern and will not be presented here for the sake of brevity. Thus we are able, by setting Q equal to unity in the above equations, to compute the profit-maximizing input demands for one unit of output given factor prices. We can combine these values of K_E, K_S, L_1, L_2, and L_3 with the values η_{ij} that determine the intermediate input requirements, giving us a production vector for use in algorithm computations.[21]

A word should be said about the factor prices. These are prices gross of all factor taxes, which are the prices faced by the producer. Later in this chapter we will explicitly multiply the tax rates by the factor prices, but the prices on the previous pages are gross of tax for simplicity.

Our assumption (1.12) of fixed input-output coefficients simplifies the computation of results a great deal. If we let the matrix (V/O) represent the matrix of input-output coefficients, while I is the identity matrix, then:

$$(1.19) \quad [I - (V/O)]^{-1} = \begin{vmatrix} h_{11} & \cdots & h_{16} \\ \cdot & \cdots & \cdot \\ \cdot & \cdots & \cdot \\ h_{61} & \cdots & h_{66} \end{vmatrix} = H$$

When we invert $[I - (V/O)]$, we derive a matrix H whose elements h_{ij} denote the output required of each industry i in order to provide one unit of output of industry j to final demand. After we have computed the primary input demands (1.16) to (1.18) we compute a vector $Q = (Q_1, \ldots, Q_6)$, where each element of Q gives us value-added for an industry. To obtain the producer prices of industry output, we multiply Q by H:

$$(1.20) \quad \text{Producer prices} = Q[H].$$

To obtain consumer prices, we multiply producer prices by the matrix Ω, which relates consumption output on the producer good classification ($i = 1, \ldots, 6$) to consumption good output ($j = 1, \ldots, 9$):

(1.21)   Consumer prices = Producer prices$[\Omega] = Q[H][\Omega]$.

Consumers face consumer prices and demand consumer goods. These demands are then translated into demands for producer goods through the Ω matrix, and industry supply is equated to demand.

Labor Input Types

In this work, one of our major interests is in examining the effects of productivity growth on factor shares and wages of different types of labor. Thus disaggregation of labor into different types is a necessity. Also, we would argue that some disaggregation of labor input is desirable given Berndt and Christensen's (1974) finding that "there is no way to construct a consistent aggregate index of blue and white collar workers in U.S. manufacturing," and that "if one wants to explain trends in factor shares, the cost of assuming aggregation is significant."[22]

The ten Census Bureau one-digit labor occupations are:

1. Professional and technical.
2. Managers and administrators except farm.
3. Clerical and kindred.
4. Sales.
5. Craftsmen and kindred workers.
6. Operatives except transport.
7. Transport equipment operatives.
8. Laborers, except farm.
9. Farmers, farm managers, farm laborers and foremen.
10. Service workers (including private household).

In order to reduce computational time, we aggregated the ten Census occupational groups into three, which are:

(A) White-collar workers — Professional and technical, managers, clerical, and sales.

(B) Skilled blue-collar — Craftsmen, operatives, and transport equipment operatives.

(C) Unskilled blue-collar — Farm, service and household workers, nonfarm laborers.

This aggregation was performed so as to minimize interoccupational mobility. Our justification for distinguishing the above three groups is simply that labor movement within the groups is greater than movements between different groups.

We must also realize that there are often large wage differentials between the different types of labor, and that some movement over time will thus take place between our labor input groups. However, since these large wage differentials do not cause enough interoccupational movement to eradicate them or to change them drastically over time, we can assume as a first approximation that workers will keep up their current rates of mobility between labor groups even if relative wages of the different groups vary somewhat from their historical pattern. Thus we are approximating the true movement of labor from one sector to another, so long as the relative wages of the various types of labor do not change too drastically.

Parameterization in the Scarf Algorithm: Production

The model which we have assumed requires choices of the parameters to be made. There are two possible means by which these parameter values may be assigned. The first is statistical estimation, and the second is a method due to Shoven and Whalley (1972), and further developed in Whalley and Piggott (1977).

In any general equilibrium model, which has been constructed in order to analyze the effects of a number of interacting policies, conventional econometric techniques may run into problems. Identification of models where demand and cost functions depend either directly or indirectly on all prices is hard, because a large number of identifying restrictions are required for any one equation to be identified. One way around this problem is to reduce the size of the model and make other simplifications in the model's structure, as has been done by Allingham (1972).

Another approach to econometric estimation is to partition the models into several different subsystems of equations. For example, a system of consumer demand functions could be estimated separately, and then the parameters estimated in this way could be used in the model. However, this approach is basically unsatisfactory since it involves inconsistent assumptions. When we partition and estimate a model in this way, we are assuming that all the variables not a part of the equations being estimated are constant. However, the econometric estimates we then obtain will be used in a general equilibrium model which explicitly recognizes the interdependence between these assumed variables and the variables in our particular subsystem of equations being estimated. Because of this inconsistency of assumption, we do not know that a model estimated in this way will generate a plausible equilibrium. It is possible that published statistics might show that the agricultural sector in the U.S. has 4% of the labor force, while a simulation using parameters estimated in this way might imply that the agricultural sector contains 20% of the labor force.

In addition, if we estimate a model that is partitioned, we must make sure that the units in which estimates are made are compatible with each other. If not, the incompatibility between parameters will lead to mistaken results. One can partially overcome this problem by trying to use unit-free parameters estimated elsewhere (such as the elasticity of substitution in a CES function), but there are often incompatibilities between published estimates and the particular model one is trying to estimate.

In light of these objections, Whalley and Piggott suggest that an identifying restriction we might use can be derived from the requirement that the economy be in equilibrium. We assume that the economy is in equilibrium for each year for which we simulate the model. This assumption can be modified to assuming equilibrium for a period of time longer than a year, which can be represented by averaging annual data, although we do not do this.

We then measure these equilibria by obtaining and adjusting data from the *National Income and Product Accounts* and other sources in a way that we will illustrate below. The observed equilibrium can be used as an identifying restriction for the parameter values that we choose. Thus the model being parameterized must be capable of generating the equilibrium dataset which was used to parameterize it. It is possible in this case to work in outside estimates of unit-free parameters such as elasticities of substitution in order to provide additional identifying restrictions on the model when the equilibrium assumption is insufficient. The parameters are obtained by solving the model's equilibrium conditions for the parameters in terms of the observed quantities and prices, and also any extraneous parameter estimates.

We should mention two additional points here. The first is that the requirement that the simulation parameters be able to generate the benchmark equilibrium dataset (the actual U.S. data over the 1947-74 period) serves as a very strong check against error, as we have found out from experience. Thus, the accuracy of our result is helped.

Secondly, our assumption of equilibrium at each point in time has great advantages, even though it may be unrealistic. If we begin at an equilibrium, change parameters, and generate a new equilibrium, we know that the differences between the two equilibria are due to the parameter changes made. If we began at a disequilibrium position, changed parameters, and generated a new equilibrium, how could we distinguish the effects of the parameter changes from the effects of movements toward equilibrium which would have occurred without any parameter changes? This problem plagues the work of Nelson and Winter (1977b), but is not a problem for our work.

Once we have decided on our estimation procedure and have obtained our dataset, we must make an assumption about the units we choose to use. The equilibrium values obtained from the data must be divided into prices and quantities. For this, the assumption which we make is that the amount of a productive factor which earns a given monetary reward (with the monetary reward given in terms of a base year) net of all factor taxes and gross of subsidies, is one unit of that factor. The data we use will be in 1967 dollars so that a unit of a factor will be defined as that amount that earns a given amount in 1967 dollars.

Since we are assuming that in equilibrium marginal revenue products of factors are equalized in all uses, industry data on payments to factors gives us our units of quantity. The amount of labor input earning $1000 base year dollars after factor taxes in any of its uses will be our unit of factor input. The same basic principle will apply to capital, with a few modifications to account for the differences between capital and labor, as discussed in chapter 3.

We can give an example of how this would apply in practice. Suppose that for the year 1967 the wage bill in agriculture was $1000 and the wage bill in manufacturing was $5000. Since both figures are in 1967 dollars, we would have one unit of labor in agriculture and five units in manufacturing.

This is a strong assumption, and we must consider what it will mean in particular cases. There are underlying physical units implied by our units defined in money terms. However, they cannot be defined. We cannot think of labor units in terms of manhours, for example, because different people have different productivity and are paid at different rates. In our previous example, if there was one manyear of labor in agriculture but only 2 1/2 manyears in manufacturing and the manufacturing labor was paid at $2000/year, while agriculture got only $1000/year, we would be saying that each agricultural manyear was only half as productive, hence was paid at only half the rate.

This units assumption is justifiable so long as the underlying assumption of factors being paid their marginal products holds. If it does not, and agricultural labor, for example, is paid at less than its marginal product, while manufacturing labor is not, then our analysis of the general equilibrium effects of productivity change will be biased. In this case, if agriculture is underpaid in this sense, then if there is movement of labor out of agriculture it will, in our model, be expressed as an expansion of the labor force. We will be assuming that this will not occur. Thus the accuracy of our simulation results will only be as strong as the underlying assumption of competitive equilibrium and marginal product pricing. We are ruling out such possibilities as discrimination and exploitation.

Example of CES production function parameterization. To see how this approach to parameterizing the model will work in practice, let us take a simple example. For a CES production function with a Hicks-neutral specification, we have:

$$(1.22) \quad Q = A\left[aK^{(s-1)/s} + (1-a)L^{(s-1)/s}\right]^{s/(s-1)}$$

We can derive the first order conditions for profit maximization by differentiating the profit identity:

(1.23) Profit $= pQ - wL - rK$

where the factor prices are understood to be net of factor taxes. If there are factor taxes they must be multiplied by w and r, e.g., $w(1+t_L)$ and $r(1+t_K)$. We then derive:

$$(1.24) \quad pA \left[aK^{(s-1)/s} + (1-a)L^{(s-1)/s} \right]^{1/(s-1)} aK^{-(1/s)} = r,$$

$$pA \left[aK^{(s-1)/s} + (1-a)L^{(s-1)/s} \right]^{1/(s-1)} (1-a)L^{-(1/s)} = w.$$

We then divide one equation by the other to get:

$$(1.25) \quad K/L = \left[wa/(r(1-a)) \right]^s.$$

It is then possible to solve for (a), the capital-labor distribution parameter:

$$(1.26) \quad a = 1.0 / \left[1.0 + (w/r)(L/K)^{(1/s)} \right].$$

Since our model operates by increasing or decreasing activities until profits in those activities are driven to zero, we may set profit in equation (1.23) equal to zero. Substituting (1.22) into (1.23), and using the value of (a) estimated from (1.26), we get:

$$(1.27) \quad A = \frac{wL + rK}{\left[aK^{(s-1)/s} + (1-a)L^{(s-1)/s} \right]^{s/(s-1)}}$$

which completely parameterizes our equation, given the assumed values of the elasticities of substitution. The same basic framework could be applied to a Cobb-Douglas function, which is a special case of (1.22) with s equal to unity.

The restriction that the parameters be such that they generate the actual equilibrium values leaves us with one degree of freedom when parameterizing the CES function, since we have three parameters minus equations (1.22) and (1.23). Since s is a unit-free parameter, we may use outside estimates of its value in the model without causing any complications.

To give a numerical example, suppose the following were the dollar values for the agricultural industry in 1967:

(1.28) $wL = 100$ $rK = 50$ $t_K rK = 50$

$pQ = 200$ $r(1 + t_K)K = 100$

(1.28) $w = r = p = 1$ $t_K = $ factor tax on K

$s = $ elasticity of substitution $= 0.5$.

Then we have as a consequence of our assumptions:

(1.29) $rK/r = K = 50/1 = 50$ $wL/w = L = 100/1 = 100$.

Our assumption that $w = r = p = 1$ means that we are dealing with data for 1967. For other years, wages and rentals net of tax will differ from unity. The assumptions on w and r determine L and K. We then have for this industry:

(1.30) $a_{1967} = \left[1 + [w/(r(1 + t_K)](L/K)^{(1/s)} \right]^{-1}$ $= 1/3$

$A_{1967} = \dfrac{wL + r(1 + t_K)K}{\left[aK^{(s-1)/s} + (1-a)L^{(s-1)/s} \right]^{s/(s-1)}}$ $= 2.66667.$

To continue the example, suppose that the following data held for agriculture in 1968:

(1.31) $wL = 110$ $rt_K K = 55$ $w = r = 1.1$

$pQ = 220$ $r(1 + t_K)K = 110$ $p = 1.0$

$K = 50$ $L = 100$ $s = 0.5$.

We then derive the following values for A_{68} and a_{68} using the same formulas as in equation (1.49):

(1.32) $A_{68} = 2.93333$ $a_{68} = 1/3$.

Thus over this period we have a 10% rise in Hicks-neutral produtivity, with no non-neutral productivity change. In the general case, however, both A and a will differ from year to year.

The values for aggregate capital and labor which we use in the above equations are found using the same basic procedure. Since we have:

(1.14) $K = [K_S]^c [K_E]^{1-c}$

and

$$(1.15) \quad L = [L_1]^{g_1} \, [L_2]^{g_2} \, [L_3]^{g_3} \quad ; \quad \sum_{i=1}^{3} g_i = 1$$

and also:

$$(1.33) \quad \frac{r_S K_S}{r_E K_E} = \frac{c}{1-c} \quad ; \quad \frac{w_1 L_1}{w_2 L_2} = \frac{g_1}{g_2} \quad ; \quad \frac{w_1 L_1}{w_3 L_3} = \frac{g_1}{g_3}$$

we may solve the above equations for c, g_1, and g_2 to get:

$$(1.34) \quad c = r_S K_S / [r_S K_S + r_E K_E]$$

$$g_1 = w_1 L_1 / [w_1 L_1 + w_2 L_2 + w_3 L_3]$$

$$g_2 = w_2 L_2 / [w_1 L_1 + w_2 L_2 + w_3 L_3]$$

Those values, along with the values of K_S, K_E, L_1, L_2, and L_3 are used in equations (1.14) and (1.15) to find overall K and L, which are then used to find the aggregate production parameters A and a.

Because the method of parameterization which we employ will determine A and a jointly, we may have some non-neutral and even non-factor augmenting technical change. We might then either have factor augmentation at two different rates, misspecification of our production functions, or Hicks-neutral change plus some non-augmenting change.

We recognize that all our results are contingent upon the parameters which we feed into our simulations. We believe that while problems of misspecification may exist, they are reduced by our methods of choosing parameters. The parameters we choose are able to exactly replicate the data used to pick them, which serves as a checkpoint against error, although it does not rule out the possibility of misspecification.

We choose a technology specification that could exhibit Hicks-neutral technical change (changes in A) in addition to possible non-neutral change (changes in "a") for several reasons. First, it is much easier to choose parameters for the Hicksian case. Allowing for the possibility of Harrod-neutral technical change requires the solution of nonlinear equations to pick parameters, if we want to be sure that the parameters can replicate the data. Secondly, we compared the changes in the distribution parameter "a" over time under the assumptions of Hicks and Harrod neutrality. Then changes in "a" were greater under the Harrodian specification in three industries and less in three others. Thus Harrod neutrality does not obviously fit the data better than Hicks neutrality.

Finally, we needed to pick a convenient functional form for our production functions to reduce computational costs. We have chosen to follow the procedures of Shoven and Whalley who have worked with this algorithm. Given our assumptions on parameterization, a 3-factor CES function gives us one degree of freedom which can be filled by outside estimates of s, a unit-free parameter. The other two parameters will vary over time to satisfy the equilibrium conditions. We could choose production functions with more parameters (such as the transcendental logarithmic). But we would then need to plug in more outside estimates of parameters which are not unit-free, or else abandon our method of estimation, which serves as a check on error. Alternative functional forms could have been chosen, but there are none that are superior overall to the one we chose. We believe that our specification of technology is preferable to others on the grounds of computational simplicity, correspondence with the facts, and conformity to previous analysis in this area.

We should note here that because all data in our model are deflated to 1967 prices, the p's in equations (1.22) to (1.31) are all equal to one. Since 1967 is our base year, the w and r values (net of factor taxes) are also set equal to unity in that year only. However, for the other years, they are not. The counterpart of the positive residual (output increasing faster than an index of inputs) is input prices increasing faster than output prices. If we have:

$$I = \text{index of aggregate input}$$
$$(1.35) \quad pQ = WI \qquad W = \text{index of input prices}$$
$$Q = \text{aggregate output}$$

then we may take logarithms and differentiate (1.24) to derive:

$$(1.36) \quad \dot{Q}/Q - \dot{I}/I = \text{residual} = 0 \text{ as } \dot{w}/w - \dot{p}/p = 0.^{[23]}$$

Thus during the period 1947-66, the data show w and r to be less than one, and for the years afterward w and r are set greater than one.

Our model is a general equilibrium model, and we do not include business cycle effects or adjustment costs in it. The economy is assumed to be always in equilibrium. However, this does not mean that our results are completely isolated from the business cycle. We derive our units of output and input from real value-added and real factor income. To the extent that these data change due to the business cycle, our measures of capital and labor input will change, as will our measures of productivity. We do not believe, however, that this will affect our results, since we have chosen a time period long enough for these effects to wash out.

The Stylized Facts of Growth and Our Model

One of the issues in the productivity growth literature is what different specifications of technical change there are, and which of these are consistent with a balanced long-run growth path, or with the "stylized facts" of long-run U.S. economic growth. These facts are:[24]

(a) The capital-labor (K/L) and output-labor (Q/L) ratios, along with the real wage (w) are rising.

(b) The output-capital (Q/K) ratio and the rate of return to capital are constant.

(c) Shares of capital (rK/pQ) and of labor (wL/pQ) are constant.

Our assumption about productivity growth is that it is Hicks-neutral, or that productivity growth does not change factor shares for a constant capital-labor ratio. This implies that the production function $F(K,L,t)$ is of the following form:

$$(1.37) \quad F(K,L,t) = A(t)G(\mathbf{K,L}).$$

Rises in $A(t)$ increase the efficiency of capital and labor at the same rate.

An alternate assumption about productivity growth is Harrod-neutrality [where the marginal product of capital is unchanged at a constant output-capital (Q/K) ratio]. This implies that the production function is of the labor-augmenting form:

$$(1.38) \quad F(K,L,t) = G(K,C(t)L).$$

Rises in $C(t)$ have the same effect as if there were more units of labor.

The problem arises because in a model with Hicks-neutral technical change, one factor share approaches zero in the long run (assuming elasticities of substitution bounded away from unity). This contradicts the stylized facts of growth. In fact, Uzawa has shown that in a one-sector growth model, the only type of technical progress which will conform to the stylized facts is Harrod-neutral (or labor-augmenting) progress.[25]

Is this a problem for our model? We do not believe so, for several reasons. First, we do not believe that the stylized facts correspond with empirical work on U.S. economic history. Denison (1954), Kravis (1959), Solow (1958), Kendrick and R. Sato (1963), and Nordhaus (1974) examine the U.S. functional distribution of income, and all of these works confirm the evidence of a strong upward trend in labor's share over time. Atkinson (1974) examines the same question for ten countries, including the U.S., with the same results. This directly contradicts one of the stylized facts of growth.

Second, because of our method of choosing parameter values, our model can replicate exactly the actual movements of U.S. economic variables over time, including labor shares. There is no contradiction or inconsistency between our model and the U.S. economic data.

Third, it is possible to test directly for the presence of Hicks or Harrod-neutral technical progress (or indeed, whether technical progress is neutral in any way). Work which has examined this question has not led to any agreement, however. Solow (1957), Kendrick and Sato (1963), Brubaker (1972), and Zind (1979) accept the hypothesis of Hicks-neutrality after various tests. R. Sato (1970) and David and Van de Klundert (1965), on the other hand, find that labor efficiency is increasing faster than capital efficiency. In other words, they postulate that:

$$(1.39) \quad F(K,L,t) = H(B(t)K,C(t)L)$$

with $C(t)$ rising faster than $B(t)$, but with *both* parameters increasing. These results are inconsistent with both Hicks and Harrod neutrality, and thus with both equations (1.37) and (1.38). Finally, Resek (1963) and Takayama (1974) also reject neutrality of either form. In summary, the empirical analysis of the form and bias of technical change has been inconclusive.

Fourth, we must also ask why the assumption of balanced growth is a desirable one. One important characteristic of postwar U.S. economic growth is large sectoral productivity growth differentials. Evidence for these differentials is provided in Nelson and Winter (1977), Kendrick (1961), and Salter (1960). Also, Baumol (1967) has developed a model using the assumption of imbalanced productivity growth, which shows sharply rising relative costs and prices in those sectors where productivity growth is slow. Many interesting questions in U.S. productivity analysis concern differential productivity growth rates between sectors and the resulting economic effects, such as those on factor shares. If as a result of productivity growth, factor shares change, we would not want to rule out such effects a priori.

Demand Function Parameterization in the Scarf Algorithm

As noted before, the demand functions used in this work are in the form of a linear expenditure system. A constant savings rate is assumed, equal to the average ratio of saving and income. However, we must determine the rest of the parameters in the demand functions: the β_i and the m_i.

We estimated income elasticities of consumption for various goods using data from the 1972-73 *Survey of Consumer Expenditures* (BLS, 1976). The estimated elasticities were used to compute the β_i from equation (1.9):

(1.9') $\beta_i = \xi_i(p_iC_i)/Y.$

The m_i parameters were computed from the demand functions:

(1.8') $m_i = C_i - \beta_i\alpha[Y - \sum_{i=1}^{n} p_im_i]$; $\sum_{i=1}^{n} p_im_i = 0$

where $(1 - \alpha)$ is the saving rate, and the parameters were then checked to make sure that, at the prevailing prices, they generated the actual consumption demands.

The advantages of this formulation are that we can impose estimated elasticities on the demand functions, that we have simple, workable demand equations, and that they satisfy Walras' law, being derived from utility functions. However, there are disadvantages, as we have previously noted.

One particular problem with our assumptions on demand is the question of whether or not it is theoretically correct to assume a constant saving rate, or in other words to treat future consumption as an aggregate. Our utility function can be regarded as a special case of a utility function defined on consumption goods at time periods $t, t + 1, t + 2, \ldots$:

(1.40) $U = U[\bar{C}_t, \bar{C}_{t+1}, \bar{C}_{t+2}, \ldots, \bar{C}_{t+n}]$

where C represents a consumption aggregate.

Liviatan (1966) shows that under certain separability conditions we can treat this function as a function of two goods (consumption and savings) and determine the consumer's budget allocation between them. Specifically, if U can be written as a separable function:

(1.41) $U = U[\bar{C}_t, H(\bar{C}_{t+1}, \ldots, \bar{C}_{t+n})]$

where H is linearly homogeneous, then the correct optimal values of consumption and capital accumulation can be determined using only C_t and H.[26] Our utility function is assumed to be separable, and so we can legitimately treat saving as an aggregate.

Government spending. In our discussion of the basic theory of the Scarf algorithm, we noted that government revenue is assumed to balance government expenditure (which requires some data adjustment) and that each consumer is given a share of total revenue. For example, this could be transfer income, welfare, etc. The shares must add to unity, but the government itself is allowed to become a consumer and to retain a share of revenue for its own consumption activities. For simplicity, we treat the government sector as spending a constant fraction of its revenue on each particular good in any particular year. This constant expenditure share assumption implies a government utility function of the form:

$$(1.42) \quad U_{gov} = U_{gov}(C_1,\ldots,C_9) = \sum_{i=1}^{9} [C_i]^{a_i} \quad ; \quad \sum_{i=1}^{9} a_i = 1$$

which is a Cobb-Douglas utility function. Alternatively, other assumptions on government spending could be considered.[27] Although the idea of the government sector having a utility function may seem unrealistic, the equivalent assumption of constant expenditure shares may not seem quite so heroic. If government is to be treated as a consumer, its demand functions must satisfy Walras' law, which they will if constant expenditure shares are used. Other assumptions could be used but no obviously better one suggests itself.

Consumption goods. We note that consumer prices are derived by multiplying producer prices by the matrix Ω, which relates consumption output on the producer good classification ($i = 1,\ldots, 6$) to consumption goods as the consumers actually demand them:

$$(1.43) \quad \Omega = \begin{vmatrix} \omega_{11} & . & . & . & \omega_{19} \\ . & . & . & . & . \\ . & . & \omega_{ij} & . & . \\ . & . & . & . & . \\ \omega_{61} & . & . & . & \omega_{69} \end{vmatrix} \qquad \sum_{i=1}^{6} \omega_{ij} = 1, \text{ for all } j.$$

$$\omega_{3j} = \omega_{5j} = 0, \text{ for all } j.$$

The rows represent output of the six industries which is sold to consumers. The structures and equipment-producing industries produce no consumption goods, so the third and fifth rows of the consumption matrix are zero. Consumer demands are defined in terms of the nine column totals, and changes in producer goods prices feed through the elements of the matrix to affect consumption. Thus a rise in the price of manufactured output by 100% would raise food prices by $100(\omega_{41})\%$, or by 56.9% for the year 1967. The derivation of the Ω matrix is discussed in chapter 2.

The row totals of the Ω matrix represent only that part of production for final demand by each industry which is sold as personal consumption. The other parts of industry final demand are gross private investment, government purchases of goods and services, and net exports. We have already dealt with government purchases and we now turn toward the determination of investment demand.

Determination of demand for investment goods. Since our model contains two types of investment goods, we must find some means of determining how to allocate savings between structures and equipment. At first, one might think that all that need be done is to channel savings into the investment good with the highest return, where return is determined as follows:

$$r = \text{rental price of capital good}$$

(1.44) $r_i = (v_i + d_i)q_i, \quad i = E,S.$ $q = \text{purchase price of capital good}$

$$d = \text{depreciation rate}$$

and where v represents the net of tax return on the capital good. The determination of these magnitudes empirically is discussed in the data chapter. When $v_E = v_S$, we simply allocate savings between structures and equipment in the same percentages as historically occurred (v in our notation). There is no capital gains term in the above equation because we are dealing with prices that have been deflated to base year (1967) prices. Thus to the extent that capital gains result from inflation, they have been removed from these prices.

Unfortunately, this simple model proved to be inadequate. Computationally, since the final computed equilibrium contains averages of price vectors which are arbitrarily close to equilibrium, but not exactly at it, the rates of return will not be exactly equal. This implies that for the final equilibrium, we will be averaging investment demands which allocate all funds into one or the other of the two investment goods, depending on the rates of return. Thus we would have no guarantee that the final investment demands are reasonably close to the equilibrium given by the data. In other words, a model of investment demands such as the one above was simply too discontinuous to be acceptable as a model of individual behavior. The accuracy of the approximation to v was not high enough using these assumptions. An assumption was needed to enable us to compute a reasonable approximation to v. Otherwise, the control solution could not be computed correctly and comparisons with alternative solutions would become meaningless.

We assumed a more continuous type of portfolio behavior. Specifically, we assumed that individuals take into account the possible variance of returns from capital in addition to the mean return. In other words, individuals are assumed to have utility functions defined on the mean return to their portfolio and on the variance of that return. We may define a portfolio as follows:

(1.45) $\kappa = \sum_{i=1}^{n} \tau_i \kappa_i$ where $\sum_{i=1}^{n} \tau_i = 1.$

The τ_i are the percentages of the ith asset in the portfolio, and the κ_i are random variables from the same distributional family (i.e., normal, Poisson, uniform). Since mean return on the portfolio (μ) is a positive good, and variance of return is a bad, we have:

(1.46) $U = U(\mu, \sigma^2)$ $U_\mu > 0, \ U_{\sigma^2} < 0.$

We may define mean return (μ) as:

(1.47) $\mu_p = \displaystyle\sum_{i=1}^{n} \nu_i \tau_i$

where the subscript p refers to the portfolio. With structures and equipment capital as the only two assets in our model, we have:

(1.48) $\mu_p = \nu_E \tau_E + \nu_S \tau_S = (\nu_E - \nu_S)\tau_E + \nu_S.$

We may define the variance of return on a portfolio (σ^2) as:

(1.49) $\sigma_p^2 = \displaystyle\sum_{i=1}^{n} \sigma_{ii}^2 \ \tau_i^2 + 2 \sum_{\substack{i=1 \\ i \neq j}}^{n} \sum_{j=1}^{n} \sigma_{ij} \tau_i \tau_j$

where σ_{ij} is the covariance of returns of the ith and jth asset, and σ_{ii} is the variance of returns on the ith asset. For a two good model, we have:

(1.50) $\sigma_p^2 = \sigma_{EE} \ \tau_E^2 + \sigma_{SS} \ \tau_S^2 + 2 \ \sigma_{ES} \ \tau_E \ \tau_S.$

Let us approximate our utility function by a linear function:

$U(\mu_p, \sigma_p^2) = a_0 \ \mu_p - a_1 \ \sigma_p^2$ (a_0, a_1 positive parameters)

$\qquad = a_0[(\nu_E - \nu_S) \ \tau_E + \nu_S] - a_1[\sigma_{EE} \ \tau_E^2 +$

$\qquad\qquad \sigma_{SS}(1 - 2 \ \tau_E + \tau_E^2) + 2 \ \sigma_{ES}(\tau_E - \tau_E^2)].$

We then differentiate with respect to τ_E and equate the result to zero to derive:

(1.51) $\tau_E = \dfrac{a_0(\nu_E - \nu_S) + 2a_1(\sigma_{SS} - \sigma_{ES})}{2a_1[\sigma_{EE} + 2 \ \sigma_{ES} + \sigma_{SS}]}$; $\tau_S = 1 - \tau_E.$

We have thus derived equations for the proportions of the average consumer's portfolio invested in equipment (τ_E) and in structures (τ_S). Since we are given

τ_E and τ_S in addition to ν_E and ν_S, we needed only to pick the other parameters $(a_0, a_1, \sigma_{EE}, \sigma_{ES}, \sigma_{SS})$ in order to generate the actual pattern of portfolio choice.

These parameters were chosen in order to give results as in figure 1.2. We assume that both structures and equipment are equally risky here. Although in principle, assets can be divided into different risk classes, there is no reason to assume that structures as a composite are riskier than equipment as a composite, and vice versa. Computations with the Scarf algorithm using this type of model were able to replicate exactly the actual percentage of funds invested in equipment and structures.

Figure 1.2

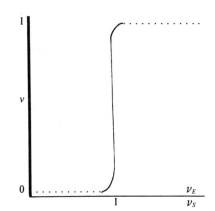

A justification for this type of model can be developed by appealing to the mean-variance analysis of Markowitz (1952, 1959) and Tobin (1958, 1969). We need a reason for an investor to diversify his portfolio. If investors simply maximize expected returns, they have no reason for diversification and instead are plungers.[28] This behavior is unrealistic. In addition, the mean-variance analysis represents a major step forward when we cannot neglect the increase or decrease in the marginal utility of wealth.[29]

There have been many criticisms of this analysis. The major problem with it is that it contains contradictions to the von Neumann-Morgenstern expected utility analysis (Fishburn 1977, Tsiang 1972, Samuelson 1967). Another problem with the mean variance analysis is that we are defining indifference curves between mean and variance which we assume to be upwardly convex, but this assumption may not always hold [see Feldstein (1969)]. Given these problems, how can we then defend a mean variance approach?

Tsiang points out that although we cannot treat the mean-variance approach as valid over all combinations of portfolios and under all conditions congruent with expected utility in the von Neumann-Morgenstern sense, we may be able to use it as an approximation. We may take utility functions which satisfy reasonable assumptions of risk and expand them into a Taylor series.[30] If the series converges quickly enough, the terms beyond the first two moments can be ignored, even if the utility function is not quadratic and the uncertain outcomes are not normally distributed. Tsiang points out that the mean-variance analysis will be a good approximation if risk remains small relative to the total wealth of the individual concerned. This wealth includes both human and nonhuman capital. Thus for most practical purposes, a fair approximation to expected utility may be obtained using only the mean and variance of returns.

Treating mean-variance analysis as an approximation over a certain range is the same type of treatment which has been used in production theory when applying the transcendental logarithmic production function. This function is not applicable over the entire range of variation of inputs, but it has still been applied in many cases, and has proved quite useful.[31] This is the justification we can offer for our assumption which is practical but which is not as theoretically desirable as other formulations.

2

Data Manipulations

Introduction

This chapter describes the adjustments which we made to the raw data sources in order to pick the parameter values for our study. This process occurs in three stages. First, we take the various data sources (*National Income and Product Accounts* and other sources) and adjust them so that the overall body of data is internally consistent and sums to common control totals. Secondly, using this consistent dataset we then choose parameters for the functions that we use (demand and production functions). Finally, in order to check the validity of the previous two steps, we plug the parameters into the Scarf algorithm and simulate it over the sample period. If there are no mistakes, this simulation will generate results equal to the original dataset used to pick the parameters. The data adjustments we make are described below.

The model which we use to represent the U.S. economy will be assumed to be in general equilibrium. Since equilibrium equations must be satisfied, the data used to generate the model's parameters must be adjusted so that it can satisfy these equilibrium conditions. For example, the total (net of factor taxes) wage payments to labor must equal the sum of all the labor income received by all the different consumers in the model. If this were not so, and it generally would not be so if the wage payment data were obtained from a different source than the labor income data, then in solving the model we would have built in a statistical error, which in turn would be implying the existence of a disequilibrium situation which did not actually occur.[1] The solution algorithm would try to adjust for this discrepancy, and might not even converge. In order to avoid this, we must make consistency adjustments to the data:

(A)   Demands must equal supplies for all products.

(B)   Total costs must equal total sales for each industry.

(C)   Each consumer group's purchases must equal disposable income for that group.

(D)   Endowments of consumers must match factor usage.

    (E)   Value of final demands (consumption + investment + government purchases + exports – imports) must equal the sum of value-added.

In addition, we must balance the government budget. In other words, total private saving equals total saving. Since the government is treated as a consumer and retains a share of revenue for its own purposes it must satisfy the same requirements each consumer must.[2]

    These consistency adjustments are needed because data derived from one source will generally not agree with data derived from another. For example, value-added data from the *National Income and Product Accounts Statistical Tables* do not agree with value-added data from the input-output tables, even though both datasets are published by the Bureau of Economic Analysis.[3] This is mainly because industry definitions differ between the two types of data. Since in our case, it was necessary to choose control totals for all the various conflicting datasets, we chose to adjust the data to the national income and product accounts whenever possible.[4] Sometimes we had to use other sources as controls, especially for total sales of an industry (equal to value added and purchases from other industries).

Control Totals: Proprietors' Income, Taxes, and Savings

The dataset which we plan to use to control the various conflicting data sources is the national income and product accounts. While these data have flaws from the viewpoint of productivity analysis, they are derived from a consistent set of definitions which is what we need. We will not use the revision of the national accounts which is employed by D.W. Jorgenson and L.R. Christensen.[5] We will work with data for the years 1947-74. For value-added data (or gross product originating—GPO) our source will be unpublished Bureau of Economic Analysis tables, revised as of June 1978. These were the latest available.

    Since we plan to use three basic factors of production (capital, labor, and materials) one major data problem is allocation of various monetary returns to the proper factors of production. This requires assumptions on the treatment of various taxes, the split between labor and capital of proprietors' income, and the various data sources to use.

Allocation of proprietors' income. One major problem in the analysis of factor shares and of productivity is the allocation of proprietors' income between labor and capital. Proprietors' income is income earned by self-employed professionals, by producers' cooperatives, and proprietors. It is composed of both labor and of capital income. The major problem is that imputing competitive returns to either capital or labor in a sector such as agriculture, where proprietors' income is a large part of total income, implies that the other factor does not earn a competitive return. Faced with this problem, there are several methods one could use to allocate this income between labor and capital. We will discuss three: the labor method, the capital method, and the proportional method.

For the labor method, one finds a wage rate from data on wages and salaries per full-time equivalent employee in a particular industry. One multiplies this by the number of full-time equivalent employees, and treats this as the labor part of proprietors' income. Of course, there are other possible wages one could choose, but the general idea is to attribute a competitive wage to labor and then assume that the rest of proprietors' income is income to capital. This has the disadvantage of implying that all the imperfections and non-competitive elements in that particular sector affect capital but not labor, since imputing a competitive wage to labor and a competitive return to capital will more than exhaust the total proprietors' income.

One could alternatively impute a competitive return to the capital stock, and multiply this by the total capital stock in that sector. This is the capital method, and it implies a much smaller return to labor than in the labor method. It also implies that all imperfections in factor markets occur only in the labor market.[6]

Our own preference is to simply allocate proprietors' income to labor by the proportion of employee compensation to national income, which was approximately 72% in 1967 (471,915 mn./655,805 mn. = .7196). Thus we assume that imperfections in factor markets affect both capital and labor income, or, in other words, there is no significant difference between proprietors' income and other income in terms of shares. This method is simple, and can be applied to NIPA data. Kravis uses this approach in his analysis of income shares. The ratio changes each year, and thus is not a constant over the whole period.[7]

Taxes. Once proprietors' income has been split into is component parts, factor taxes on labor and capital income must be determined. We are assuming that the relevant return from the viewpoint of the factor owner is his net return, net of factor taxes which vary from sector to sector, but gross of income taxes and transfers. Income taxes which do not vary sectorally will be assumed not to affect the sectoral allocation of factors.

We will be using the convention that one unit of a factor is that amount which earns $1000 of return net of factor taxes but gross of income taxes. Thus to define the economy's endowment of capital and labor, we need to know what taxes are factor taxes on which factor.

The taxes and factor payments which we consider to be labor factor taxes are:

(A) Employee contributions for social insurance;

(B)   Employer contributions for social insurance;

(C)   "Other labor income" as defined in the *National Accounts*. This is mainly employers' contributions to private pension funds.[8]

Both B and C are part of the employers' cost of hiring a particular worker, and thus will be treated as factor taxes on labor. This is of course a simplification, but it does not necessarily imply any particular economic incidence. However, our treatment does differ from that of Christensen and Jorgenson, who consider the social security system part of the private national economy. We assume social insurance to be a governmental activity.[9]

The taxes which we consider to be taxes on capital income earned in a particular sector are:

(A)   the corporate income tax;

(B)   the property tax.

It is not obvious that the property tax is a tax on capital income. For a defense of this position, see Mieskowski's treatment of the property tax.[10] There is also the problem of large regional and local differences in property tax rates. We will assume a uniform property tax overall, and ignore these differences.

Thus, we are assuming that for six sectors (agriculture, structures-producing, manufacturing, equipment-producing, services, and a residual industry, where these sectors are aggregated from data for ten industries) there are factor tax rates for labor and capital, and that these sectors possess a certain number of homogeneous units of labor and capital which are used to produce output. We do not consider different rates of taxation of different firms in a sector, and thus do not explicitly model the corporate-noncorporate business split, unlike Shoven and Whalley, for example.[11]

The output taxes on each sector are thus the taxes which have not been allocated specifically to labor and capital. Thus, total sectoral indirect business taxes (IBT) including business transfer payments, but not including property taxes are allocated to the various sectors, and the tax revenue from each is used to derive an ad valorem tax rate on output for each sector. Indirect business taxes includes many taxes which have differing impacts, but these taxes will be abstracted from here.[12] Business transfers, which are largely bad debts, will be considered to be taxes. In other words, the economic model by itself will not determine them.

There are many problems with this treatment (some taxes are not ad valorem, and rates differ between states). However, we believe that is is a useful simplification to average tax rates between geographical areas and to set marginal and average rates equal. The complexity of the actual tax system makes some simplification necessary, and we are not using this model to determine tax incidence. Some other works which do attempt to model the incidence of taxation also make these simplifying assumptions [see Shoven and Whalley (1972), and Whalley (1977)].

Once the value-added numbers and labor and capital inputs have been found, the next need is the specification of total output by industry (output before subtraction of materials inputs). The numbers we use for industry total output are obtained from the Office of Economic Growth, Bureau of Labor Statistics.[13] We use the BLS data except for manufacturing, where we adjust it to conform to the sum of value-added and intermediate goods from the input-output tables.

Treatment of saving and income distribution. In my model we must specify the ownership of all the commodities by consumers, who, in the aggregate, must own the entire stock of each commodity in the economy. We will assume that all consumers are the same, and that they own the capital and labor in the economy. This assumption does several things:

(A) We do not have to specify different consumption functions for richer or poorer consumers.

(B) We do not have to analyze the differential factor ownership by income class.

While this assumption does violence to reality, it does avoid the problem of the specification of the size distribution of income. The relationship between the functional and the size distribution would have been required to be completely specified in order to find each consumer's income, and the data problems here are immense. The loss of realism is more than compensated for by the gain in ease of finding the data for the algorithm. In addition, there is some evidence that in general equilibrium models disaggregation on the production side is much more important than disaggregation on the consumption side, and that not much is gained by modelling more than one type of consumer.[14] Whalley (1977a) in a simulation disaggregates a hypothetical economy with factor market distortions and examines the effects on the national income from removing these distortions. He shows that increased numbers of consumers and changes in functional forms for their demand functions affect estimates of efficiency losses very little, compared to disaggregation on the production side. The changes in estimates of efficiency losses are also very small when compared with the variation in efficiency loss estimates between the distorted and non-distorted cases. This is an example of the importance of the index number problem.

Since the consumers in the aggregate must own all the capital stock, and since this model has no true financial sector, we must treat corporate retained earnings and capital consumption allowances the same way as personal savings. Thus our data for disposable personal income ($Y = C + S$) will not match the disposable personal income figure in the NIPA data, although the consumption figures will be identical. Table 2.1 compares the numbers that we will use with their counterparts in the NIPA data from which they were derived.

Table 2.1.   Comparison Between Our National Accounting Framework and the NIPA Statistical Tables for 1967

	Our Numbers	NIPA Numbers
GNP	796312	796312
National Income	748165	655805
Personal Income	703474	626626
Disposable Income	620534	544548
Personal Consumption	490358	490358
Personal Saving	130176	40869

Reconciliation with National Income and Product Accounts

Total economy. Table 2.1 shows our breakdown of the gross national product by the major categories we use, and also compares them with the official national accounts numbers. The main results of our assumptions on GNP can be seen in the table. The main reason for national income, personal income, disposable income, and personal saving totals being greater under our classification scheme than in the actual NIPA tables is our treatment of capital consumption allowances and undistributed profits. Because we work with a model with no true financial sector, and because the consumers in this model must own the capital stock, we include these as part of personal saving and national income, personal income, and disposable income. Overall GNP and consumption totals match between the two data sources.

One other major difference also occurs. Since we treat property taxes as a factor tax on capital, it belongs in national income. This is because "national income is the incomes that originate in the production of goods and services attributable to labor and property supplied by residents of the United States. Thus, it measures the factor costs of goods and services produced ..."[15] and so property taxes as a factor cost must be included. This is in contrast to the national accounts treatment, which does not include them in national income.

Government. Our government budget will also not be identical with the government budget from the NIPA's. We combined state and local government units with the federal government to make one large governmental sector. We did not believe that the benefits of disaggregation here were worth the cost. In addition, the following chart shows the GNP components that were added to the government sector. Since the SLCS of government enterprises (if negative) results in lower prices of products or subsidies of other types, and these losses must be made up through government revenues, we felt justified in adding this to the governmental sector. Business transfers which are largely bad debts, will also be treated as taxes, and thus will be an exogeneous variable, not determined by the model. According to the NIPA explanation, "... they fit into the general category of transfer payments, which are defined as payments to persons for which the latter do not perform current services."[16]

Expenditures	*Receipts*
1. Personal transfers to foreigners	1. Personal transfers to foreigners.
2. Subsidies less current surplus of government enterprises (SLCS).	2. Other labor income (mainly payments into pension and welfare funds).
3. Business transfers.	3. Business transfers.
4. Benefits paid by private pensions, supplemental unemployment benefits, workman's compensation.	

Personal transfers to foreigners were moved into the government sector, since they represent a wedge between disposable income and the sum of consumption and savings. In order to avoid estimation of a demand function for this good, we simply treat it as a tax. It is as if the government acted as an intermediary between the private sector and foreigners. The same simplification is applied to other labor income, which consists mainly of payments for pensions and welfare funds.[17] The benefits paid by these funds are also included in the government sector since they resemble transfer payments.

Thus, for 1967 the government sector will look as in the following table. Since the government often runs a deficit or surplus, violating the consistency assumptions listed at the beginning of this chapter, we must adjust government expenditures or taxes or both in order to balance the budget. In a Walrasian general equilibrium model of the type we have here, the data must be constructed so that the equilibrium conditions of the underlying model are satisfied. If (in the data) taxes do not match government expenditure, or if expenditures by households do not match household disposable income, or if the value of gross industry input is not equal to the gross value of industry output, then in solving the model prices, outputs and inputs will be adjusted so as to try to overcome this gap. We then may get a situation where instead of the correct amount (say 4%) of workers in the agricultural sector, the model may allocate 15% of workers to agriculture, if it converges at all.[18]

Table 2.2.   Receipt and Expenditure Items Included in the
Government Sector, 1967

Receipts ($mn)		Expenditures ($mn)	
Corporate profits taxes	32480	180188	– Purchases of goods and services
		(85142)	– (employee compensation)
Contributions for social insurance	43385	(95046)	– (other goods)
(employer)	(22774)		
(employee)	(20611)		
Indirect Business Taxes	70239	8908	– Net interest paid
Personal Taxes and Nontaxes	82078	49458	– Transfers to persons
Receipts of pension funds	21651	17265	– Workmans compensation, benefits paid by pension funds, etc.
Business transfers	3137		
		3108	– Transfers to foreigners
Personal transfers to foreigners	862	(862)	– (personal)
		(2246)	– (governmental)
Total	253832	263683	– total
		-9851	– government deficit

Also, in this situation we would not know that the simulation effects we find when we change our productivity parameters are a result of the changes in parameters. This is a problem that affects the work of R.R. Nelson and S.G. Winter. Since they initiate their simulation work with their model in a disequilibrium situation, they are unable to separate the effects of their model tending toward equilibrium from the effects of parameter changes.[19]

The convergence results of the algorithm apply for an equilibrium which exists. However, any set of data picked at random does not necessarily represent an equilibrium. Our assumption that the economy is in equilibrium means that consistency adjustments must be made to the data to enable them to represent an equilibrium.

In this work, we adjust government expenditures (federal, state, and local including social insurance funds) to balance the overall government budget. It may be objected that this treatment is unrealistic. It is. The other option we have is to create a financial sector to allow for borrowing and inflationary effects. None of the other work using the Scarf algorithm has done this and we do not do so either. Without a method of treating the government deficit financially, we must interpret the financial transactions of the government sector as real transactions, and thus we must eliminate the deficit in order to ensure that our dataset represents an equilibrium. Instead of adjusting expenditures, we could adjust taxes, or both. Here we follow Whalley's work but this is a matter of preference. However, without a financial sector, the government deficit must be eliminated.

Labor and Capital Returns by Industry

We have described in the previous pages the determination of gross labor and capital income in the total economy. The next step is to find out how these returns break down by the six industries (and also government) which we are using. We need to find a gross labor and gross capital income in a particular industry, against which the factor taxes are applied in order to derive the net labor and capital income in that industry. Since all the gross income, factor tax, and net income figures are either available by industry or can be easily approximated, this is easily done. We then need to relate the net incomes of labor and capital to the endowments of labor and capital and the allocation of factors between industries.

The convention we will use is that the total endowment of labor and capital units (in the economy and in each industry) is equal to the net labor and capital income in 1967 prices in that industry. In other words, for a particular year, X dollars of labor income in 1967 prices in a particular industry means that there are X labor units employed in that industry. This assumption has been used by Shoven and Whalley in their use of the Scarf algorithm.[20] It has the advantage of enabling the algorithm to reproduce the actual gross and net factor incomes and factor taxes which will pertain in the equilibrium of any particular year. By choosing units for factor endowments based on 1967 prices, endowments of labor and capital in a particular industry for any year can be varied so that when these endowments are input into the algorithm, the actual data which would be consistent with these endowments at that time period can be generated. This serves as a check on error and also helps to parameterize a model with many parameters.

To give one example, suppose the following data represent the situation for labor income in the total economy in the years 1966, 1967 and 1968 after the gross and net incomes and factor taxes have been converted to 1967 dollars by dividing by the GNP deflator:

Table 2.3. Example of Determination of Total Units of Labor in Our
Economy for a Hypothetical Situation

Value	1966	1967	1968
Gross Labor Income	85.0	110.0	135.0
Factor Taxes	5.0	10.0	15.0
Net Labor Income	80.0	100.0	120.0
Price of Labor(w)	0.90	1.00	1.10
Units of Labor(L)	88.9	100.0	109.1

The above figures are all in 1967 dollars. Of course, the price of labor is shown as rising here. This is because (as discussed in chapter 3) rises in productivity are equivalent to rises in input prices relative to output prices. Since 1967 is our base year, we set the price of labor equal to unity in that year. Then our convention is that one unit labor is that amount which earns $1 in 1967 prices. This gives us 100 units of labor for that year. In equation form:

$$(2.1) \quad 1967 \quad wL = 100 \quad w = 1.0 \quad L = 100.$$

For 1966 and 1968, the price of labor differs from 1.0, but we apply the same convention:

$$(2.2) \quad 1966: \quad wL = 80 \quad w = 0.9 \quad L = 80/0.9 = 88.9.$$

$$(2.3) \quad 1968: \quad wL = 120 \quad w = 1.1 \quad L = 120/1.1 = 109.1$$

For the other years (1947-74) we apply the same methods. For each individual industry, the process is the same with a common overall labor price being applied. For capital input which will be discussed later, the situation is more complicated.

This convention does have some peculiarities. Thus it may happen that in a recession year net labor or net capital income may decline overall. By our conventions, this will mean that the labor or capital stock will be considered to decline if net labor or net capital income does. Thus our measures of inputs are more input usage than input stock measures. Also, we are employing three different types of labor input in this model. However, we will apply a common price of labor when performing the above calculation. Thus differences in wages between labor inputs will translate into differences in endowments.

Capital Input Data

We plan to use two types of capital in this work as inputs into the production process: structures and producers' durable equipment. So far, the data we have derived have been for total capital. To use structures and equipment, we need to do two things. First, data on gross and net capital incomes and capital factor taxes must be split into separate figures for structures and equipment. Secondly, we must determine the proper treatment of residential structures, changes in inventory stocks, land, and consumer durables.

Consumer spending on durable goods in principle could be treated as investment in capital goods, and a separate consumer durable capital stock measure and depreciation rate computed. However, we do not do this for two reason. The first is for the sake of simplicity. Secondly, there is more and better information on structures and equipment than on consumer durables. Thus consumer durable spending will be treated as being equivalent to other consumption.

Inventory changes will be treated as an exogeneous final demand category (the other final demand categories are personal consumption expenditure, government purchases, and private fixed investment). The alternative would be to treat inventory change as an intermediate good. We follow national income and product accounting procedure by treating inventory change as a final demand component, since we are using national accounting data as control totals and thus are following the conventions used in constructing these tables.[21]

Residential structures in the private sector will be aggregated to form one stock, which will be treated as an input in the real estate sector, as is the case in the national accounts. We will also not treat land as a separate capital good, since less complete information is available about it.[22] We will, however, disaggregate our capital income and capital price measures sectorally, therefore explicitly allowing for different rates of corporate income taxation and property taxation by sector.

Because the national income accounts do not show a split of property income by the particular type of property which generates than income, property income must be split into its various components (in this case, structures and equipment.) The work by Christensen and Jorgenson (hereafter C-J) provides an example of how to do this.[23] We plan to use their corporate sector formulas to determine capital stock prices and incomes since each of our industries contains some corporations. By varying the corporate income and property tax rates sectorally the change in the corporate-noncorporate mix can be accounted for.

Structures–equipment property income split. We can reproduce the Christensen-Jorgenson formulas for the determination of rental prices for corporate producers' durable equipment (subscript E) and corporate structures (subscript S). The sole purpose of these equations is to enable us to impute the returns to structures and equipment capital stocks. These equations are as follows:[24]

$$(2.4) \quad E: \quad r_E = [1 - (z_E)\, t_{corp} - t_{cred} + y] / [1 - t_{corp}]$$
$$\times (v + d_E) q_E + t_{prop}(q_E)$$

or, multiplying by the equipment stock:

$$(2.4') \quad E: \quad r_E K_E = [1 - z_E t_{corp} - t_{cred} + y] / [1 - t_{corp}]$$
$$\times (v + d_E) q_E K_E + t_{prop} q_E K_E$$

and:

$$(2.5) \quad S: \quad r_S = [[1 - z_S t_{corp}] / [1 - t_{corp}]] (v + d_S) q_S$$
$$+ t_{prop} q_S$$

or, multiplying by the structures stock:

$$(2.5') \quad S: \quad r_S K_S = [[1 - z_S t_{corp}] / [1 - t_{corp}]] (v + d_S) q_S K_S$$
$$+ t_{prop}(q_S K_S)$$

where:

t_{prop}	=	corporate property tax rate;
v	=	net return after tax on corporate property;
t_{corp}	=	corporate income tax rate;
d_E, d_S	=	depreciation rates;
t_{cred}	=	investment tax credit;
y	=	$t_{cred}(t_{corp}) z_E$ for 1962, 1963, zero otherwise due to changes in tax law (Christensen and Jorgenson, (1969), pp. 304-5);
q_E, q_S	=	asset prices;
r_E, r_S	=	rental prices;
z_E, z_S	=	present value of depreciation deductions on capital.

In (2.4') and (2.5'), $r_E K_E$ and $r_S K_S$ are total equipment capital income and total structures capital income, respectively. Also, $t_{prop}(q_E K_E)$ is total property tax payments on equipment, and $(\nu + d_E)q_E K_E$ is equipment capital income after deduction of income and property taxes. We have deflated all income flows to constant 1967 dollars, and thus we neglect capital gains terms which would otherwise occur here. The above equations are only versions of the following equations that have taxes included in them:

$$(2.6) \qquad r_E = (\nu + d_E)q_E \qquad r_S = (\nu + d_S)q_S;$$

$$(2.6') \qquad r_E K_E = (\nu + d_E)q_E K_E \qquad r_S K_S = (\nu + d_S)q_S K_S.$$

This can be seen by setting $t_{prop} = t_{corp} = t_{cred} = 0$ in (2.4), (2.4'), (2.5), and (2.5'). These equations serve to determine rental prices, given tax rates, depreciation rates, depreciation deductions (z_E, z_S), stocks of capital (K_E, K_S), and the return on capital.

Jorgenson and Christensen point out that for their application of their method we must have two additional equations to solve for ν and t_{corp}. The rest of the above terms are available from various data sources. These equations are as follows:[25]

$$(2.7) \qquad \text{Sector property income} = \sum_{i=1}^{n} p_i K_i \quad ; \qquad \begin{aligned} n &= \text{number of capital types} \\ p_i &= \text{rental prices} \end{aligned}$$

$$(2.8) \qquad \text{Corporate income taxes} =$$

$$t_{corp} \left[\begin{array}{l} \text{property income } - \text{ property taxes} \\ - \text{ present value of depreciation deductions.} \\ - (t_{cred} - y)(\nu + d_E)q_E K_E \end{array} \right]$$

We solve these equations for ν and t_{corp}, and plug these values into our rental price equations to derive our structures and equipment property income split.

The data sources for these calculations are as follows. For q_E and q_S, we use the implicit price deflators for producers' durable equipment (PDE) and for structures from the NIPA.[26] We then derive the stocks of PDE and structures using the perpetual method with investment from NIPA, depreciation from Christensen and Jorgenson (1969), and capital benchmarks from Goldsmith.[27] Since we need sectoral stocks of equipment and structures, we spread the gross stocks of PDE and structures using the percentages of producers' durable equipment and structures held by each sector in unpublished net stock data from the Office of Economic Growth, Bureau of Labor Statistics. The above stocks are all in real terms. The sectoral property tax rates (t_{prop}) will be set equal to the ratio of the value of property taxes to total value of capital in a sector. Finally, the values for z_E, z_S, d_E, t_{cred}, and y will come from Christensen and Jorgenson (1969).[28]

Application to algorithm. In the previous section, we have seen how gross and net of tax equipment and structures rentals can be computed from overall capital gross and net of tax rental incomes. The only purpose of using the Christensen-Jorgenson formulas was to make this split. These data are not yet in quite the right format for use in the Scarf algorithm. For the algorithm, we need tax rates that are ad valorem tax rates on the rental prices of equipment and structures which will not be the same as those defined in the previous section. In addition, the convention we are using in this work, as mentioned previously, is to define a unit of capital as that amount which generates a certain amount of rental income. Given our capital rental income data, we can define stocks of capital suitable for inclusion in the algorithm that will enable the algorithm to reproduce the actual data values of any particular equilibrium. In this section, we will define the service prices (r_E and r_S) as being net of tax prices. Gross service prices will be multiplied by one plus the tax rate.

To give an example, let a unit of equipment capital be defined as that amount which produces $0.10 of equipment income net of tax (in 1967 prices). Suppose that a particular sector in any particular year has $10000 of gross equipment income measured in 1967 prices, $1000 of corporate income tax on equipment and $1000 of property tax on equipment, that the equipment depreciation rate is 0.05, and that the after-tax return to capital is 0.05. The Christensen-Jorgenson formulas have been used to find what amount of total tax is assessed on structures and on equipment. We may define the asset price of a unit of equipment as equal to $1.00 (in 1967 dollars). Then (assuming that there are no expected capital gains), we have:

$$(2.9) \quad r_E K_E = 8000 \qquad r_E t_E K_E = 2000 \qquad r_E(1 + t_E)K_E = 10000$$

from the above data. We also have:

$$(2.10) \quad t_E \;\; = .25 = \$2000/\$8000 \text{ (from the above data)}$$
$$r_E \;\; = \$0.10 \text{ (by assumption)}.$$

This then implies:

$$(2.11) \quad r_E K_E/r_E = \$8000/0.10 = 80,000.$$

There are then 80,000 units of equipment capital in that sector. This method of finding the capital stocks and tax rates given capital incomes satisfies the Scarf algorithm criterion that the ad valorem tax rate (plus one) times the net service price of the input equals the gross service price, or that gross of tax property income equals net property income times (the tax rate plus one):[29]

(2.12) $(1 + t_E)r_E K_E = \$10000 = (1.25)(0.10)(80,000).$

For a justification of this, see Shoven and Whalley (1973), who show that the algorithm requires "for each production activity...there is an associated producer tax vector $T^j = (t_{1j}, \ldots, t_{nj})$ whose components are the ad valorem tax rates applying to inputs and outputs when the jth activity is utilized."[30]

For our work, tax rates will vary between sectors, but (ν) will not, since otherwise investors would want to disinvest from sectors or assets with lower rates of return and invest in sectors (or assets) with higher rates, implying that the original situation was not an equilibrium. It might be objected that this is not so if there is risk aversion, and sectors with lower rates of return have lower risk. We choose in this work to assume that the riskiness of all sectors and types of capital are the same. The sole function of the portfolio choice analysis is to give us *continuous* demands for investment goods, rather than massive investment and disinvestment in equipment or structures resulting from minute changes in rates of return. In addition, there is no reason to believe that at the aggregated level at which we are working structures or equipment have markedly different riskiness.

A brief note on the treatment of capital gains is in order. Because the units convention we will use implies that a dollar value becomes a real value (since asset prices of capital are set equal to unity), use of deflated values to pick parameters is imperative. As far as the C-J rental prices are concerned, it makes no difference whether we find nominal rental prices using nominal magnitudes and then deflate, or deflate the nominal magnitudes first and then find real rental prices, as long as the correct deflators are used. Our preference would be to deflate the asset price first, since then we can use the NIPA implicit price deflators, and ignore the capital gains term in the normal price of capital equation.

Labor Input Data

In addition to analyzing the effects of technical change on labor in general, we would like to see how technical change has affected different occupational categories of labor differently. Labor can be cross-classified by many characteristics, such as education, occupation, industry, sex, race, age, employment status, etc. However, we will not consider sex, race, age, education, or employment status (self-employed or not). For this paper, workers who are of different sexes, races, ages, educational levels or employment status (self-employed or not) but who earn the same amounts of labor income will be treated as equivalent amounts of labor. However, occupational and industry differences will be considered.

We will assume that labor inputs are mobile between different industries. However, we will not assume that they are mobile over different occupations. If labor inputs are immobile between occupations, each occupational group which is distinguished becomes a different type of labor. The occupational groupings which are most commonly distinguished are listed below (although we will not maintain this level of detail in our work):[31]

1. Professional and technical
2. Managers and administrators
3. Sales workers
4. Clerical and kindred
5. Craftsmen
6. Operatives
7. Transport equipment operatives
8. Laborers except farm
9. Farm workers
10. Service and household workers

When computing with the Scarf algorithm, different types of labor will have different prices. Since computational time increases with the square of the number of goods (at least), aggregation of labor types is desirable.[32] In addition, aggregating occupational groups that have high interoccupational mobility will tend to make the other occupations more distinct.

We plan to use data developed by Gollop and Jorgenson on labor input. Their data gives information on labor input for the years 1947-74, and cross-classifies it by education (5 levels), industry (51 industries), occupations (10), sex, age (8), and employment status (self-employed or not), for a total of 81,600 types of labor for each year that the data are available.[33] We will reaggregate their data to use only some of the industry and occupational detail.

Occupational breakdown. The occupational breakdown we plan to use is threefold:

(A) White-collar workers — Professional and technical, managers, clerical, and sales.

(B) Skilled blue-collar — Craftsmen, operatives, and transport equipment operatives.

(C) Unskilled blue-collar — Farm, service and household workers, nonfarm laborers.

Ideally, one would like to aggregate those occupations between which mobility is high, and distinguish between those which have little interrelationship. There is some evidence on interoccupational mobility for the ten groups listed in the previous section from the 1970 Census. These data classify the major occupational groups of workers in 1970 by their major occupational group in 1965. It is then possible to try different groupings of the ten different occupations in order to minimize interoccupational mobility. After trying different occupational combinations, we found that the classification above gave us the lowest interoccupational factor mobility. Our justification for distinguishing the above three groups is simply that labor movement within the three groups is greater than the movements between different groups.

Two qualifications must be kept in mind when working with this Census data, however. First, although we can obtain a matrix cross-classifying workers by occupation in 1965 and 1970, transition probabilities based on such a matrix are not meaningful, because the population has been growing. In order to derive the true transition probabilities between different occupations, M.A. King shows that it would be necessary to adjust for changing population size and also to make several other adjustments.[34] Thus the interoccupational labor movement in the Census data may overestimate or underestimate the true probability of transition between occupations. We use the data in spite of this problem since it is the best available.

Secondly, when we examine the Census data, one point which stands out is that there is a great deal of interoccupational mobility, and also movement into and out of the labor force. Leigh (1978) shows that while some occupational mobility over the 1965-70 period is within the same one-digit occupational category (for example, within the professional and technical group), much mobility is between Census groups:

Table 2.4. Occupational Mobility: Percentage of Workers with a Different One-Digit Occupation in 1970 and 1965

Age	Percent
25–34	35.6%
35–44	22.0%
45–64	16.7%

Steinberg (1979) shows that of men aged 35 to 45, only 70% to 76% (depending on whether the initial sample year was 1960 or 1970) of the men employed in the sample year (1960 or 1970) were continuously employed in each of the five following years, while the corresponding figures for 20-year-old women were only 27% to 31%. A good deal of this mobility is into and out of the labor force rather than between occupations, but we can see that there is a great deal of labor mobility in the U.S. economy. The actual labor data that we use have this occupational mobility built in to a certain degree. We have attempted to reduce this, but we must admit that some movement does take place over time between our labor input groups. It is hard to aggregate the ten listed occupational groups into three or four larger groups in such a way that more than 70% of workers in each group kept the same occupation from 1965 to 1970. For example, in the grouping which we will use, 91.5% of all white-collar (WC) workers in 1965 were still WC in 1970, and 86.3% of skilled blue-collar (BC) workers in 1965 were still in the same grouping in 1970, but only 68.1% of non-farm laborers and household and service workers in 1965 were still in the same types of jobs in 1970. But we would argue that more is gained than is lost by disaggregating labor, especially in view of Berndt and Christensen's (1974) findings on the impossibility of creating a consistent aggregate index of blue- and white-collar workers in U.S. manufacturing.

Actual labor data. The actual labor data that we will use come in two parts:

(A)   Real and nominal total labor compensation by industry division from the national accounts. Real compensation is determined by deflating nominal compensation by the output price for that sector.

(B)   Data developed by Frank Gollop and Dale Jorgenson which gives compensation, employment, and hours worked of labor for 51 industries, ten occupations, eight age groups, five educational levels, and which also classifies it by sex and employment class.

Arriving at an industry division by occupation breakdown means that we must aggregate across age, education, sex, race, and employment class groups. Since we will be using the convention that a unit of labor is that amount which earns $1000, we need only use compensation data. However, since the compensation numbers are in nominal terms, we need a deflator to find real compensation. This deflator will be used to convert the nominal compensation into real compensation in 1967 dollars. It will be determined as nominal compensation divided by average weekly hours. This should be quite accurate because it is adjusted for most of the possible determinants of earnings. We will use the national income and product data as control totals. These computations will provide us with a complete breakdown of labor input by industry and occupation controlled to NIPA definitions, which is the labor data we will use.

Industry Interrelationships: Input-Output, Final Demand, and Personal Consumption Expenditure by Industry

Input-Output Data

The total effect of productivity change on an economy (discussed in chapters 1 and 4) not only operates through increased output and saving leading to increased capital accumulation, but also through expansion in intermediate input other than capital, as Hulten points out (1978). Thus to properly analyze the induced accumulation effect, we must create a model which takes these interrelationships into account. This section discusses our attempts to do this.

The four major input-output tables available to us at the time of this computation were the 1947, 1958, 1963, and 1967 input-output tables.[35] These I-O tables distinguish 87 separate industries, including 52 different manufacturing industries. In order to reduce computational costs and deal with a less complex model, we aggregated the interindustry transactions and final demand data. We created six different industries: agriculture, manufacturing, structures-producing, equipment-producing, services, and others.[36] We explicitly distinguish a structures and an equipment sector since we will distinguish structures and equipment capital stocks and determine their growth over time in our model.

To account for the possibility of manufacturing productivity growth differing from other industries' growth we retain the manufacturing sector. The agricultural sector is also retained. We would like to see whether rises in agricultural productivity and shifts of labor out of agriculture into other sectors have made an important positive contribution to American economic growth. The conventional viewpoint is that reallocation of resources from farming was an important source of productivity growth in the U.S.[37] We would like to incorporate this possibility into our model. The rest of the industries (besides services and capital-producing ones) are aggregated into a residual category.

To see how these data fit together, we can examine figure 2.1. Interindustry transactions are given in the first six rows and columns of the figure, and the intermediate row and column totals are given in the next row and column. Moving left to right, the next four columns represent final demand by industry. The derivation of the data in these columns will be discussed further below. Consumption here is classified by industry, and it must be related to consumption classified by type of good.

One data need which is made obvious by this figure is the need to specify total output for each industry (output before subtraction of interindustry purchases). The numbers we will use for industry total output are obtained from the Office of Economic Growth, Bureau of Labor Statistics. We use the

BLS data except for manufacturing, where we use the sum of GPO and intermediate goods from the I-O tables.

Figure 2.1

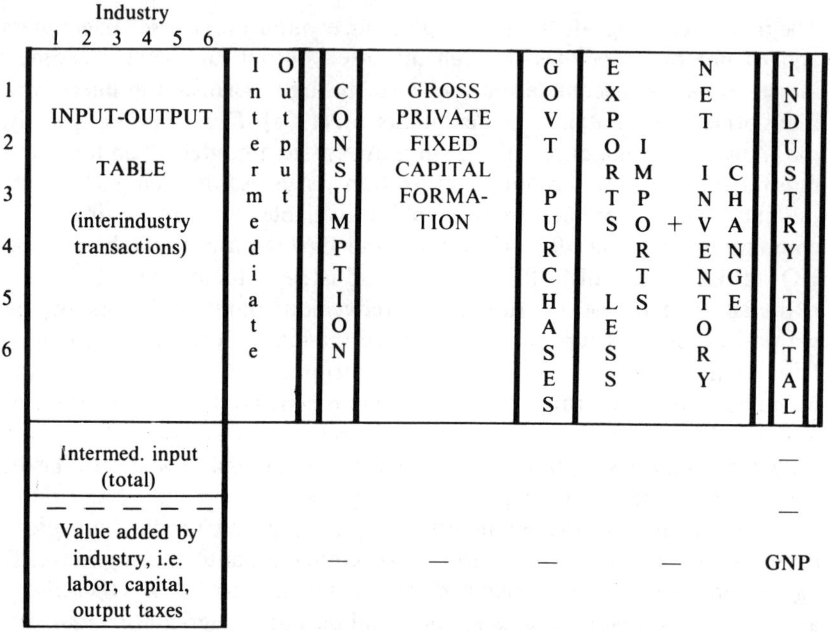

	Industry 1 2 3 4 5 6	Intermediate output	CONSUMPTION	GROSS PRIVATE FIXED CAPITAL FORMA-TION	GOVT PURCHASES	EXPORTS IMPORTS LESS	+	NET INVENTORY CHANGE	INDUSTRY TOTAL
1 2 3 4 5 6	INPUT-OUTPUT TABLE (interindustry transactions)								
	Intermed. input (total)							—	—
	Value added by industry, i.e. labor, capital, output taxes		—	—	—	—		GNP	

Industry final demand. Four final demand categories will be considered as can be seen from the previous figure: personal consumption expenditure (PCE), gross private fixed capital formation, government expenditures, and a residual final demand category, made up of net exports and net inventory change which balances total final demand for each industry and its component parts. The consumer in the model will demand the consumption goods, the private savings in the model will be invested in the fixed capital, and fixed shares of government revenue will be spent on each of the goods.

Gross private fixed capital formation is a category of final demand, and consumers will be assumed to invest savings in structures and equipment. The input-output matrix includes interindustry transactions in materials, semi-finished goods, and services from one industry to another. However, sales of capital goods from the capital-producing industries are included in final demand only, and not in intermediate input. Although industries do buy and sell capital goods, the national income accounting convention is that this activity is part of final demand, and this is how we treat it.

The residual final demand category will be handled by introducing an exogeneous amount of domestic and foreign ownership of resources. This is a way of taking into account the Scarf algorithm restriction that imports minus exports must equal domestic ownership of foreign resources minus foreign ownership of domestic resources.[38] Some researchers working with the Scarf algorithm have constrained exports to equal imports, thereby leading to other inaccuracies in the data since the consistency adjustments applied to the data require equal changes elsewhere to satisfy the criteria listed at the beginning of this chapter.

Adjustments using the RAS model. The major adjustments that were made to the data which we use in this work were adjustments to make a given matrix conform to a new set of control totals. For example, we know the values of the 1958 input-output table. But we need to find the I-O table for 1959, given only total output, value-added, and final demands by industry. In other words, we have a set of values for a matrix, and want to use our prior information on 1958 values and row and column totals for 1959 to estimate the I-O table for 1959. Adjustments such as this were necessary for the I-O tables, and for the matrix relating personal consumption by type of product to PCE by industry division.

There is a model which can be used to estimate these matrices, although it is not statistical in the usual sense. This model is known as the RAS model, or the biproportional matrix model.[39] Suppose that we know the value of a matrix A in a particular year. Suppose in addition that for another year we only know the row sums u_i $(i = 1, \ldots, n)$ and column sums v_j $(j = 1, \ldots, m)$ where $\Sigma u_i = \Sigma v_j$. Assuming that the matrices have not changed radically from one period to another, we want to use our information on A to estimate the matrix in the alternate year.

Michael Bacharach discusses how to apply the RAS model in his paper (1965).[40] If r and s are column vectors, we can consider the following process:

(2.13) $A_1 = r'A$;

(2.14) $A_2 = A_1 s = r'As$

where $r_i = u_i \Big/ \sum_{i=1}^{n} a_{ij}$ and $s_j = v_j \Big/ \sum_{j=1}^{m} a_{ij}$

and the elements a_{ij} are elements of A. After deriving A_2, we check to see whether the process has converged, or in other words whether the old matrix is controlled to the new row and column totals (u_i and v_j). If not we continue the process by replacing A with A_2, and perform the multiplication process again.

This process has several properties:[41]

(A) A positive element of A can never vanish in the process.

(B) A solution of the process is unique.

(C) The process will converge to a unique solution under very general conditions.

To take a simple example, let A equal:

$$(2.15) \quad A = \begin{vmatrix} 1.0 & 1.0 \\ 1.0 & 1.0 \end{vmatrix}, \ u = (30,70), \text{ and } v = (40,60).$$

Then $r = (15,35)$, and $s = (0.8,1.2)$. The process converges after one iteration, and A_2 now equals:

$$(2.16) \quad A_2 = \begin{vmatrix} 12 & 18 \\ 28 & 42 \end{vmatrix}$$

In practical applications of this model, it was necessary to employ two different convergence criteria, in order to avoid excessive computation time for convergence. First, when each of the row and column factors had converged within an arbitrarily small distance of unity (0.0001), the algorithm was considered to have converged. In addition, when the maximum change of any one element of A from one iteration to the next was less than a small percentage (0.1%) the process was also considered to have converged.[42]

Input-output table computation. Since the 1947, 1958, 1963, and 1967 I-O tables are available, and we need data on the intermediate years and years after 1967, we estimated I-O tables for each year between 1947 and 1974. First, each value in the intermediate years was determined by linear interpolation, and other adjustments were made to make the I-O tables conform to each other.[43] Then, using our total output, final demand, and value-added data (in real 1967 dollars), we derived a data series for intermediate output for each industry in real terms for this time period. We then applied the RAS model to the I-O tables to ensure that each I-O table for each year conformed to the control totals. The results was a series of input-output tables for the years 1947-74, deflated to 1967 prices.

Definition of Structures and Equipment Industries

Because our capital input data will consist of structures and equipment inputs, we need to define a structures-producing and an equipment-producing industry. This requires data on expenditures for structures and equipment, classified by industry.[44]

The basic source of data on investment in structures and equipment by industry is the Bureau of Economic Analysis's book *Interindustry Transactions in New Structures and Equipment, 1963 and 1967.* Since our gross fixed private capital formation data (GPFK) from the NIPA's includes some additional amounts besides new structures and equipment (such as sales of existing structures and equipment and dealer commissions on these sales), we spread these across the industry totals derived from the above volume. Although this assumption may be slightly inaccurate, both of these categories are included in gross private fixed investment in the *National Accounts,* and since we are using the *National Accounts* figures as control totals, we follow their procedure here. The amounts involved are quite small (less than 1%) of the total investment.

The computations performed lead to the table below relating gross private fixed capital formation in structures and equipment to those industries from which the capital formation came. The structures and equipment totals sum to the NIPA totals for the year 1967.

Table 2.5. Fixed Capital Formation by Industry, 1967 ($mn.)

Industry	Structures	Equipment	Totals
Construction	54067.	–	54067.
Manufacturing	1002.5	45352.4	46354.9
Transportation	–	803.	803.
Communication	–	1062.	1062.
Trade	271.	6078.6	6349.6
Finance, Insurance and Real Estate	2089.5	4.	2093.5
Totals	57430.	53300.	110730.

Similar tables are derived for 1947, 1958, and 1963, with structures and equipment totals matching the NIPA totals. For the intervening years, we linearly interpolate values for structures and equipment investment for each industry, and control these to the NIPA totals for that year.

Once we have data on structures and equipment investment by industry, we aggregate all structures and equipment producing firms together using the fraction of each industry division's final demand which it sells to other industries as structures and equipment. For example, if the communications sector sells 5% of its final demand output as equipment in 1970, then 5% of the labor, capital, and materials inputs are aggregated into the equipment producing industry. Doing this for each industry then gives the data for two out of our total of six industries.

Personal Consumption Expenditures (*PCE*)

Because consumers do not consume the output of each industry, but instead demand consumption goods (food, clothing, housing, etc.) we needed to build a bridge between consumption by types of goods and by industry divisions. For example, in 1967 one dollar spent on food led to 4.5 cents spent directly on the output of the agriculture industry, 56.6 cents spent in manufacturing, and 38.9 cents spent in other industries. The matrix we used to build this bridge relates the data types listed in table 2.6. This matrix is the Ω matrix discussed in chapter 1. We define it as:

$$(2.17) \quad \Omega = \begin{vmatrix} \omega_{11} & . & . & . & \omega_{19} \\ . & . & . & . & . \\ \omega_{61} & . & . & . & \omega_{69} \end{vmatrix} \quad \begin{array}{l} \sum_{i=1}^{6} \omega_{ij} = 1 \text{ for all } j \\ \\ \omega_{3j} = \omega_{5j} = 0, \text{ for all } j \end{array}$$

where each entry is the amount of ith industry final demand that goes into the production of the jth consumption good. The data for this were obtained from the *NIPA Statistical Tables* and from the input-output tables for the years 1947, 1958, 1963, and 1967. Thus we have values of Ω for these four years and need to estimate the matrix for the in-between years. The other intermediate values were determined by linear interpolation, and were adjusted to NIPA totals. Because actual entries of these matrices did not add to the row and column totals from the *NIPA Statistical Tables,* the RAS model was applied to them. Use of this matrix enables us to relax the assumption, otherwise necessary, that consumers demand the output of industries such as trade directly.

Table 2.6.   Consumption Table: Classification of Consumption Goods by
Types of Product and by Industry Division

A) Types of Product	B) Industry Division
1. Food	1. Agriculture
2. Clothing	2. Structures-producing
3. Personal care	3. Manufacturing
4. Housing	4. Equipment-producing
5. Household operation	5. Services
6. Medical care	6. Other
7. Personal Business	
8. Transportation	
9. Other consumption, consisting of: Recreation, Private Education Religious and welfare activities Foreign travel and other	

3

Simulation Results

Simulations and Reasons for Performance of Different Runs

The simulation model which has been developed in the previous chapters is quite flexible. We can simulate any possible rate of Hicks-neutral productivity change by varying the parameter (A) in the following equations:

$$(3.1) \quad Q = A[aK^{(s-1)/s} + (1 - a)L^{(s-1)/s}]^{s/(s-1)} \quad \text{(Hicks-neutral)}.$$

After choosing parameters for the Scarf algorithm as discussed in chapter 1, we can simulate the productivity growth process using different assumptions on the productivity growth rates.[1]

We perform a simulation by picking a rate of growth for the Hicks-neutral technical change parameter in each industry $(\dot{A}/A)$ and making no other changes in the parameters. We treat technical change as exogeneous throughout this analysis, so we are justified in varying this parameter without regard to what the rest of the economy is doing. One example of the assumptions we make is a run where we set $(\dot{A}/A)$ equal to zero for agriculture and let $(\dot{A}/A)$ equal the values estimated from the data for the other industries. The simulation results then tell us the effects of a zero rate of Hicks-neutral productivity change in agriculture on the economic variables of the system, given the validity of our assumptions.[2]

When we change one or more industry rates of productivity change, there will be effects on the functional distribution of income in addition to changes in input and output quantities. We can then determine which productive factors benefit and which lose from productivity change in a particular industry. Finally, we can find the effects of productivity change on capital formation and intermediate output by comparing the control run with the alternate solution.

What we are doing here can be seen in the following diagram. First we perform our control run (run 1) which tracks the actual data exactly by plugging our parameters into the Scarf algorithm. We then change one or more parameters for each alternative simulation, and then simulate the economy's path over the 1947-74 period, using the Scarf algorithm as our solution mechanism for the model. This gives us a value for any particular variable of interest, say X_a. We can then compare X_a and X_c at the final period. Generally we compare end period values, or growth rates of X_a and X_c over the whole period. When we use the terminology "actual situation," "actual data," or "control run," we are speaking of X_c.

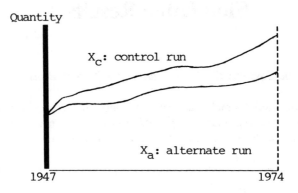

The following runs were performed using different assumptions on the rates of Hicks-neutral productivity change:

(1) $\dot{A}/A$ = actual values for all industries (control solution).

(2) $\dot{A}/A = 0$ for all industries. This run will, in comparison with the control run, show what the induced accumulation effects of productivity change are.

(3) $\dot{A}/A = 0$ in agriculture, no other parameter changes.

(4) $\dot{A}/A = 0$ in construction (structures-producing industry) with no other parameter changes.

(5) $\dot{A}/A = 0$ in manufacturing, no other parameter changes.

(6) $\dot{A}/A = 0$ in the equipment-producing industry, no other parameter changes.

(7) $\dot{A}/A = 0$ in services, no other parameter changes.

(8) $\dot{A}_i/A_i = \dot{A}_j/A_j = e$ for all $i,j = 1, \ldots, 6$. e here is set equal to the constant average rate or productivity change for the overall economy. This is computed as:

$$e = \dot{Q}/Q - \dot{I}/I, \quad \text{where} \quad \begin{aligned} Q &= \text{index of overall value-added} \\ I &= \text{index of overall input, and} \end{aligned}$$

$$\dot{Q}_t/Q_t = \sum_{i=1}^{6} w_t[\log(Q_{it}) - \log(Q_{i,\ t-1})]$$

$$w_t = (1/2)[Q_{it} \Big/ \sum_{i=1}^{6} Q_{it} + Q_{i,\ t-1} \Big/ \sum_{i=1}^{6} Q_{i,\ t-1}]$$

$$\dot{I}_t/I_t = \sum_{i=1}^{5} M_t[log[I_{it}] - \log(I_{i,\ t-1})]$$

$$M_t = (1/2)[I_{it} \Big/ \sum_{i=1}^{5} I_{it} + I_{i,\ t-1} \Big/ \sum_{i=1}^{5} I_{i,\ t-1}]$$

This formulation is the discrete, or Theil-Tornquist[3] approximation to the Divisia index.

(9) $\dot{A}_i/A_i = \dot{A}_j/A_j = e/2$ for all $i,j = 1,\ldots, 6$. e is as above. This simulation thus gives each industry one half the constant rate of productivity change.

(10) $\dot{A}_i/A_i = 0$ after 1965 for all industries, with productivity before then being set equal to the actual values.

(11) $\dot{A}_i/A_i$ for 1965-74 = $\dot{A}_i/A_i$ for 1947-65. In other words, this run has no productivity slowdown in it. The rates of productivity growth prevailing pre-1965 were applied to the post-1965 period.

(12) A projection using the 1972 production parameters, with appropriate productivity change, and applying then to the period 1973-78. This run was done to see how the model predicted outside the sample period.

The reasons why we performed the runs we did are as follows. The first run, or control solution, was necessary in order to check whether the model could replicate the data used to pick the parameters. If it could not, then we could not be sure that differences between the actual data and alternative simulations were due to the particular parameters we chose to change.[4] However, the control solution was able to track the actual data, so we were assured that the productivity parameters we changed in runs 2 through 12 were the sole cause of differing results.

The other simulations (runs 2-12) which we performed can be divided into four major groups as follows.

(A) Run 2—No productivity change in all industries.

(B) Runs 3-7—No productivity change in one and only one industry.

(C) Runs 8-11—The results of different assumptions on productivity change for all industries are explored. These assumptions show what would have happened if there was no dispersion in productivity growth rates between industries, and if the productivity slowdown either had occurred in a more exaggerated fashion or had not happened at all.

(D) Run 12—Projecting the movement of the economy to 1978. This run is to check the ability of the model to predict outside the sample period.

The most important run performed was run 2. This is because the major reason motivating this study was to verify the existence and measure the magnitude of the induced accumulation effect, as reported by Hulten (1975, 1978, 1979). This effect, in short, is the extra capital accumulation and intermediate output induced by increased output and savings due to productivity change, and occurs because growth of capital and intermediate input cannot be considered exogenous. We examine this effect by comparing the actual data for the U.S. economy in the 1947-74 period with what would have happened if no productivity change had occurred. The differences between the two situations (runs 2 and 1) give us the magnitude of the induced accumulation effect. It is the confirmation of this effect which is one of the two major results of this work. While the other runs are important, this run is the most interesting.

The second major reason for performing run 2 was to show the total effect of productivity change on the distribution of factor income. By comparing a zero productivity change solution with the actual data, the differences in labor and capital factor incomes and shares can be found, and thus the incidence of productivity change on the distribution of income can be found. This is the other major result of this paper.

The second groups of runs (3-7) each held productivity change to zero in only one industry. The total general equilibrium effects of this one productivity change led to large intersectoral shifts in factor inputs and to changes in the composition of output. The motivating factor behind this group of simulations was the desire to analyze the effects of agricultural productivity change. Agriculture is the industry with the highest rate of productivity change over our sample period. However, agricultural output did not increase at the same rate as agricultural productivity. This then led to large transfers of labor and capital out of agriculture and into other industries. In order to see what the situation would have looked like without this strong agricultural technical progress, we ran one simulation (run 3) with zero productivity change in agriculture.

The other runs (4-7) in group B followed along the same lines. Although the other industries did not have quite the same high productivity growth rates as occurred in agriculture, some of them (e.g., manufacturing and services) were quite a bit larger. Thus reducing their rates of productivity change often has quite a large impact on overall capital accumulation, on the functional distribution of income, and on the sectoral allocation of factors. These runs also helped us to explore the properties of the model.

Runs 8-11 let us examine the effects of different assumptions on the rates of growth of productivity for several industries at once. One issue which has received much attention is that of differences in productivity growth between industries.[5] We can examine the effects of this interindustry dispersion in productivity growth by contrasting the actual data (run 1) which exhibit dispersion with simulations where all industries manifest the same growth in efficiency. There are three runs which do this. Run 8 gives each industry the economy-wide average rate of growth of productivity, while run 9 gives each industry one half the average rate. Finally, run 2 gives each industry zero productivity change. One would expect that there would be strong similarities between the results of these three runs. This is in fact what we find. The intersectoral factor reallocations show similarities, although the capital accumulation is markedly different.

The other runs in this group examine the effects of the productivity slowdown after 1965. Run 10 examines what the economy would have looked like without any productivity change post-1965. Run 11 maintains the rates of growth of productivity that occurred in the 1947-65 period after 1965, thus eliminating the productivity slowdown. This run is interesting, since we can find out by examining it what would have happened if there had been no productivity slowdown, and thus determine now much the productivity slowdown has cost us in lost output.

Run 12 is in a class by itself. The purpose of this run is to find out how well the model predicts outside the sample period by starting in 1972 and simulating until 1978. The ability of the model to predict the course of the economy during the energy crisis, higher inflation, and the productivity slowdown will help us to evaluate its accuracy when shocked by changes in the rates of productivity growth.

Zero Productivity Change Simulation Effects

We will examine the effects of our assumption of zero productivity change on the economic variables in our model and compare the results of this simulation with the actual data. There are many variables of interest here, such as the capital-labor (K/L) and output-labor (Q/L) ratios and the growth in input and output prices and quantities in this run. In addition, the effects of productivity change on the sectoral allocation of factors will be examined.

Capital-labor (K/L) *and output-labor* (Q/L) *ratios in production.* We define the capital-labor ratio as:[6]

$$(3.2) \quad K/L = K_1^{c1} K_2^{c2} \Big/ [L_1^{g1} L_2^{g2} L_3^{g3}] \qquad \begin{array}{l} c1 + c2 = 1 \\ g1 + g2 + g3 = 1. \end{array}$$

The output-labor ratio, or labor productivity, is defined as:

$$(3.3) \quad Q/L = Q \Big/ [L_1^{g1} L_2^{g2} L_3^{g3}] .$$

In table 3.1, we compare the values of the simulations (runs 2 and 1) at the end of the twenty-seven year period in which the model was simulated (1974) for the K/L and Q/L ratios. Run 1 represents the actual data. The numbers in the table are not percentage changes over time. We are taking the final year results of these runs, and computing the number:

$$[X_{run\ 1,\ 1974} - X_{run\ 2,\ 1974}] / X_{run\ 1,\ 1974}.$$

K/L ratios in run 2 decrease strongly, and more strongly in this run than in any other runs because here we have assumed the largest decreases in productivity change of any of the runs performed.

Table 3.1.   Comparison of 1974 (End-of-Simulation Period) Values Between Run 2 and the Control Solution

% Differences in Values: $[X_{run\ 1,74} - X_{run\ 2,74}]/X_{run\ 1,74}$

Industry	K/L ratio	Q/L ratio	Total Factor Productivity
Agr.	−43.6	−73.6	−196.2
Misc.	−43.9	−59.3	−85.2
Constr.	−63.7	−48.6	−62.0
Manuf.	−49.0	−49.2	−68.5
Equip.	−46.5	−49.7	−71.5
Serv.	−44.6	−47.1	−73.1

The output-labor ratios or labor productivity tend to change in close association with the rates of Hicks-neutral productivity change.[7] For a constant elasticity of substitution production function with Hicks-neutral productivity change, the following relation holds:

$$(3.4) \quad \dot{Q}/Q - \dot{L}/L = \dot{A}/A + M_K[\dot{K}/K - \dot{L}/L] + s[M_K - a][\dot{a}]/[a(1 - a)]$$

where M_K is equal to capital's share, and the other parameters are exactly as in (3.1). Thus the rate of change of the Q/L ratio is the sum of the rate of total factor productivity growth, a term involving the rate of change of the K/L ratio, and a term involving the change in a, the capital-labor distribution parameter. The last term is generally small in relation to the others. We can see from the above table that the major determinant of Q/L is $\dot{A}/A$, the rate of total factor productivity change. For example, Q/L decreases most strongly for agriculture and miscellaneous industries, whose rates of growth of productivity are reduced the most by our assumption of zero productivity change.

The assumption of zero productivity change in all sectors leads to substantial changes in the allocation of capital and labor inputs by industry. Table 3.2 shows the percentage changes in units of capital between the alternate and the control solution for the final year (1974) of both runs. We can see that although capital input decreased in each sector in the simulation as opposed to the actual situation, the percentage decreases differed strongly between industries. The decreases in capital input tended to be inversely related to the decreases in rate of growth of overall productivity change. Thus we can see that agricultural capital input decreased the least relative to the control solution, while agricultural total factor productivity growth decreased the most. On the other hand, construction capital input decreased the most, while construction productivity growth fell the least compared to the control solution. The reasons for this are not hard to discover. We can derive input demands for overall capital and labor as follows:

$$(3.5) \quad K = (Q/A)\,[a + (1 - a)[r(1 - a)/(wa)]^{s-1}]^{s/(1-s)};$$

$$(3.6) \quad L = (Q/A)\,[(1 - a) + a\,[wa/(r(1 - a))]^{s-1}]^{s/(1-s)}.$$

Differentiating the capital demand equation, we get:

$$(3.7) \quad \dot{K}/K = \dot{Q}/Q - \dot{A}/A + [\dot{w}/w - \dot{r}/r]XY(1 - s)(1 - a)$$
$$+ [\dot{a}]X[1 - Y(1 - a - s)/a]$$

where:

$$(3.8) \quad X = [s/(1 - s)]\,[Q/(AK)]^{(1-s)/s}$$
$$Y = [r(1 - a)/(wa)]^{s-1}$$

and where the coefficient of the $(\dot{w}/w - \dot{r}/r)$ term is positive. Capital demand decreases most strongly in those industries such as construction where the decrease in productivity is small relative to the decrease in output. Since, in addition, the price of labor falls relative to the price of capital, we have capital-labor substitution as one reason for the large falls in capital input. On the other hand, in agriculture, the extremely large fall in productivity growth induced by our assumptions leads to approximately the same demand for capital, even though total economy gross output has fallen by 55%, and the economy-wide endowment of structures and equipment has fallen by 37% and 45%, respectively.

Table 3.2.   Comparison of 1974 Capital Input and Total Output Between Run 2 and Run 1

(% Diff. in End-of-Period Values=[$X_{\text{run } 1,74} - X_{\text{run } 2,74}$]/$X_{\text{run } 1,74}$

Industry	VARIABLE			
	Overall K	Structures	Equipment	Total Output
Agric.	-4.0	4.7	-6.3	-55.1
Misc.	-37.9	-36.1	-42.8	-55.0
Constr.	-77.6	-76.4	-78.9	-68.3
Manuf.	-54.9	-50.9	-56.1	-55.2
Equip.	-41.7	-36.7	-43.3	-45.2
Serv.	-56.5	-53.4	-58.3	-58.5
Overall		-37.4	-45.1	-55.3

We can see this same result in a slightly different manner. We may rewrite (3.4) as:

$$(3.9) \qquad \dot{Q}/Q = \dot{A}/A + \dot{I}/I + [s/(a(1-a))][\dot{a}]$$

where:

$$I = H(L,K) = \text{overall input index}$$

$$(3.10) \quad \dot{I}/I = M_K(\dot{K}/K) + M_L(\dot{L}/L) \; ; K = K(K1,K2) = \text{capital index}$$

$$L = L(L1,L2,L3) = \text{labor index}$$

We can neglect the last term in (3.9), since it will generally be small in relation to the other terms. Thus we see that if output does not change drastically, a large fall in rates of total factor productivity growth will force increases in overall input into the industry with the largest productivity declines. This pattern holds true in this run, and also in those runs where only one industry's rate of productivity change is held to zero.

For labor inputs the situation is slightly different than for capital inputs. In our work, we assume that changes in labor supply are exogenous, and thus the supply of labor is invariant under our assumptions on productivity change. The same determinants affect the sectoral demand for labor as affect the demand for capital. Those sectors (agriculture, equipment-producing, and miscellaneous industries) which had reductions in productivity growth that were much greater than the falls in output attracted labor inputs relative to those sectors (construction, manufacturing, and services) where output fell more than productivity growth. So under our assumption that technical change is exogenous, the total effect of technical change was that of forcing labor out of agriculture and into manufacturing, services, and construction.[8]

Table 3.3 shows percentage changes in units of labor between this run and the control solution. In this case the overall price of labor fell relative to that of capital, but the price of unskilled labor fell least, leading to decreases in demand for unskilled labor in all sectors except agriculture, which is intensive in the use of unskilled labor.

Table 3.3.   Comparison of 1974 Labor Input Values Between Run 2 and Run 1

(% Diff. in End-of-Period Values=$[X_{run\ 1,74}-X_{run\ 2,74}]/X_{run\ 1,74}$

Industry	Types of Labor			
	Total	White-collar	Unskilled	Skilled Blue-Collar
Agric.	70.1	91.5	67.5	102.9
Misc.	10.6	10.4	-3.4	17.0
Constr.	-38.3	-39.9	-47.5	-36.3
Manuf.	-11.7	-13.6	-24.5	-8.5
Equip.	9.0	7.2	-6.2	13.6
Serv.	-21.6	-19.9	-30.0	-15.2

Another way of describing what is occurring in this simulation is table 3.4 which shows annual percentage growth rates of capital and labor, and differences between the growth rates.

We can also compute aggregate input as a function of capital and labor from the equation:

$$(3.11) \quad I = [aK^{(s-1)/s} + (1-a)L^{(s-1)/s}]^{s/(s-1)}.$$

Aggregate input growth rates are given in table 3.5.

Table 3.4. Average Annual Percentage Growth Rates of Capital and Labor, 1947-74, and Percentage Differences in Growth Rates

Rates $=\log[X_{74}/X_{47}]/27$ % Diff $=[\text{Rate}_{\text{run 1}}-\text{Rate}_{\text{run 2}}]/\text{Rate}_{\text{run 1}}$

Ind.	Capital			Labor		
	Run 2	Run 1	% Diff.	Run 2	Run 1	%Diff.
Agric.	1.12	1.27	-11.9	-0.81	-2.78	-70.9
Misc.	2.27	4.03	-43.8	1.33	0.95	39.2
Constr.	-3.79	1.76	-315.4	-0.79	1.0	-178.2
Manuf.	-0.49	2.46	-119.8	0.47	0.93	-49.6
Equip.	0.67	2.67	-74.8	1.43	1.11	28.9
Serv.	-2.33	0.76	-407.3	0.69	1.59	-56.5

Table 3.5. Average Annual Percentage Growth Rates of Total Input, 1947-74, and Percentage Differences in Growth Rates

Rates $=\log[X_{74}/X_{47}]/27$ % Diff $=[\text{Rate}_{\text{run 1}}-\text{Rate}_{\text{run 2}}]/\text{Rate}_{\text{run 1}}$

Ind.	Simulated (Run 2)	Control (Run 1)	% Difference
Agric.	-0.57	-1.66	-65.6
Misc.	1.80	2.36	-23.7
Constr.	-1.27	1.23	-203.4
Manuf.	0.33	1.34	-75.4
Equip.	1.30	1.49	-12.9
Serv.	0.55	1.74	-68.5

We can see that the total effect of productivity change was to redirect inputs toward the three industries (construction, manufacturing, and services) where productivity change was less than the average. Productivity change led to greatly increased capital accumulation, which was directed to the industries with lower productivity change. For example, the total effect of productivity change on capital input in construction was to make it grow 315% faster than it would have otherwise. The corresponding figure for labor input is 178%. However, for labor input the negative percentage difference between growth rates in the two runs is misleading. The total impact of productivity change in agriculture was to force labor input out of agriculture, as the lower growth rate in the control solution shows.

Total output and intermediate input. We have discussed previously the induced reallocation of factor input between sectors due to productivity change. However, there is another aspect to the impact of productivity change on a sector. Increases in productivity affect intermediate input, which then serves to magnify the effect of technical change. Table 3.6 shows the growth rates of total output, intermediate input, and value-added by industry over the sample period for the zero productivity run and the control solution. Since gross output is equal to the sum of intermediate input and value-added, we have:

$$(3.12) \quad \dot{O}/O = (\dot{V}/V)[V/(V + Q)] + (\dot{Q}/Q)[Q/(V + Q)]$$

where O is gross output, V is intermediate input, and Q is value-added. This states that the growth rate of gross output is a weighted average of the growth rates of intermediate input and value-added. Computing the percentage differences between the final years in both the simulated and the control solution gives us table 3.7.

Table 3.6.   Average Annual Percentage Growth Rates of Gross Output, Intermediate Input, and Value-Added, 1947-74, and Percentage Differences in Growth Rates

Rates $=\log[X_{74}/X_{47}]/27$			% Diff $=[\text{Rate}_{\text{run }1} - \text{Rate}_{\text{run }2}]/\text{Rate}_{\text{run }1}$					
	Gross Output			Intermediate Input			Value-Added	
Ind.	Run 2	Run 1 % Diff.		Run 2	Run 1 % Diff.		Run 2	Run 1 % Diff
Agr.	-.87	2.10	-141	-.86	2.72	-131	-.88	1.15	-176
Misc.	0.87	3.83	-77	.65	3.87	-83	.96	3.81	-75
Const	-1.51	2.74	-155	-1.36	2.59	-152	-1.88	3.05	-162
Mfg.	0.16	3.13	-95	0.24	2.93	-92	0.01	3.45	-100
Equip	1.11	3.33	-67	1.14	3.09	-63	1.05	3.67	-71
Serv.	0.39	3.64	-89	1.23	4.08	-70	-.31	3.32	-109

Table 3.7.   Comparison of 1974 Gross Output, Intermediate Input, and
Value-Added by Industry Between Run 2 and Run 1

(% Diff. in End-of-Period Values=$[X_{run\ 1,74}-X_{run\ 2,74}]/X_{run\ 1,74}$

Ind.	Gross Output	Intermediate Input	Value Added
Agr.	−55.1	−61.9	−42.2
Misc.	−55.0	−58.0	−53.6
Const.	−68.3	−65.6	−73.6
Mfg.	−55.2	−51.7	−60.6
Equip.	−45.2	−40.9	−50.6
Serv.	−58.5	−53.7	−62.5

The changes in output composition resulting from productivity change do not seem to follow the same pattern as the changes in productivity. This is because of the interaction of changes in demand and changes in productivity.

Producer prices. One would expect that changes in producer goods prices between runs 2 and 1 would be directly related to rates of technical change. Rises in output per unit of input are equivalent to rises in input prices relative to output prices, since:

(3.13) $P[Q] = W[I]$ and $A = Q/I = W/P$;

(3.14) $\dot{A}/A = \dot{Q}/Q - \dot{I}/I = \dot{W}/W - \dot{P}/P$

Thus run 2 should show output prices increasing most in those industries that formerly exhibited the highest productivity growth rates. This is in fact what we find. There is a substantial correspondence between the percentage changes in producer prices and the productivity growth rates computed on a value-added basis, with not quite as much of a correspondence between the price changes and the gross output residuals. But we can see that a major determining factor of producer price change is the rate of growth of productivity.

We should note the effects of these producer price changes on consumer goods prices. Table 3.9 shows the end-of-period percentage differences between consumer prices in runs 1 and 2.

There is not as large a range between the smallest and the largest consumer price increases (68.5-93.5%) as there is between the largest and smallest annual

Table 3.8. Average Annual Percentage Growth Rates of Producer Prices and Productivity, 1947-74

Rates = $\text{Log}[X_{74}/X_{47}]/27$

	Run 2		Run 1 - Annual Rates of Prod. Growth+			
			Total output		Value-added	
Ind.	Prod. Prices	Rank	Base	Rank	Base	Rank
Agr.	3.581	1	1.1193	1	2.8093	1
Misc.	2.502	2	0.9947	2	1.4487	6
Const.	1.789	5	0.5879	6	1.8264	4
Mfg.	1.941	4	0.8002	5	2.1125	3
Equip	1.944	3	0.9137	3	2.1752	2
Serv.	1.783	6	0.9060	4	1.5784	5

+ Total output base: If $O = A'G(V,K,L)$, where O is gross output, V is intermediate input, then $\dot{A}'/A' = \dot{O}/O - M_V'(\dot{V}/V) - M_L'(\dot{L}/L) - M_K'(\dot{K}/K)$. M_V', M_K', M_L' are gross output shares.

Table 3.9. End-of-Period Percentage Differences in Consumption Goods by Type of Product Between Run 2 and Run 1

Consumption Good Type	Percentage Differences $[X_{\text{run } 2,74} - X_{\text{run } 1,74}]/X_{\text{run } 1,74}$
Food	85.2
Clothing	80.1
Personal Care	73.2
Housing	93.5
Household operation	84.1
Medical care	68.5
Personal Business	86.8
Transportation	79.7
Recreation, education and foreign travel	74.0
Overall	83.3

producer price increases (1.783-3.581). This is because each consumption good is composed of several different producer goods, and the consumer and producer good classification is related through a fixed coefficient matrix. For example, in 1974, the composite good food was composed of 59.5% manufacturing output, 5.1% agricultural output, and 35.4% from other industries. Thus a doubling of the price of agricultural output could only raise food prices by 5.1%.

Input prices. We compute aggregate input prices from individual input prices according to the following equations:

$$(3.15) \quad w = [w_1/g_1]^{g_1} [w_2/g_2]^{g_2} [w_3/g_3]^{g_3} \; ; \; L = [L_1]^{g_1} [L_2]^{g_2} [L_3]^{g_3} \; ;$$

$$(3.16) \quad r = [r_1/c_1]^{c_1} [r_2/c_2]^{c_2} \; ; \; K = [K_1]^{c_1} [K_2]^{c_2}$$

and:

$$(3.17) \quad wL = w_1[L_1] + w_2[L_2] + w_3[L_3] \; ;$$

$$(3.18) \quad rK = r_1[K_1] + r_2[K_2]$$

Differentiating (3.15) and (3.16), we get:

$$(3.19) \quad \dot{r}/r = c_1[\dot{r}_1/r_1] + c_2[\dot{r}_2/r_2] + \dot{c}_1(\log[r_1/c_1] - \log[r_2/c_2]) \; ;$$

$$(3.20) \quad \dot{w}/w = g_1[\dot{w}_1/w_1] + g_2[\dot{w}_2/w_2] + g_3[\dot{w}_3 w_3] + \dot{g}_1(\log[w_1/g_1]$$
$$- \log[w_3/g_3]) + \dot{g}_2(\log[w_2/g_2] - \log[w_3/g_3]) .$$

Our index of aggregate input price is:[9]

$$(3.21) \quad W = [a^s r^{1-s} + (1 - a)^s w^{1-s}]^{1/(1-s)} .$$

Differentiating equation (21) for overall input price W gives:

$$(3.22) \quad \dot{W}/W = a^s r^{1-s}[\dot{r}/r]/W + (1 - a)^s w^{1-s}[\dot{w}/w]/W + [\dot{a}/a][s/(1 - s)]Z$$
$$\text{where } Z = a^s r^{1-s} - w^{1-s}(1 - a)^{s-1} a .$$

Thus the change in aggregate input price is composed of three terms: one which gives the effect on W of changes in capital price r, one term showing the effect of changes in labor price w, and one term that shows the effect of changing parameters. The changes in labor and capital prices result from changes in the individual input prices and changes in parameters. In the above equations, r_1, r_2, w_1, w_2 and w_3 include all taxes on inputs. Since the parameters g_i and c_i differ by industry, so will an overall capital and labor price. Table 3.10 shows the average annual percentage changes in overall capital and labor input prices by industry for runs 1 and 2.

Table 3.10. Average Annual Percentage Growth Rates in Capital and Labor Prices, 1947-74, and Percentage Differences in Growth Rates

Rates = $\text{Log}[X_{74}/X_{47}]/27$ | % Diff=$[\text{Rate}_{\text{run 2}}-\text{Rate}_{\text{run 1}}]/\text{Rate}_{\text{run 1}}$

| | Capital | | | Labor | | |
Ind.	Run 2	Run 1	% Diff.	Run 2	Run 1	% Diff.
Agr.	2.871	0.77	274	2.699	3.42	-21
Misc.	2.022	0.13	1426	1.41	2.58	-45
Const.	2.783	0.81	245	0.91	2.17	-58
Mfg.	2.54	0.44	479	1.44	2.69	-46
Equip.	2.60	0.52	404	1.47	2.70	-45
Serv.	3.04	1.00	205	0.96	2.04	-53

Table 3.11. Average Annual Percentage Growth Rates of Aggregate Input Prices, 1947-74, and Percentage Differences in Growth Rates

Rates = $\text{Log}[X_{74}/X_{47}]/27$ | % Diff=$[\text{Rate}_{\text{run 2}}-\text{Rate}_{\text{run 1}}]/\text{Rate}_{\text{run 1}}$

Ind.	Run 2	Run 1	% Diff.	Capital Share in Run 1.
Agr.	3.27	2.81	16	0.406
Misc.	1.66	1.45	15	0.459
Const.	1.18	1.83	-35	0.191
Mfg.	1.62	2.11	-24	0.212
Equip	1.70	2.18	-22	0.213
Serv	0.93	1.58	-41	0.134

These price changes result from the prices of the original labor and capital types changing in the following way:

Table 3.12.   Comparison of 1974 Input Prices by Input Type Between Run 2 and Run 1

(% Differences in 1974 Values = $[X_{run\ 2,74} - X_{run\ 1,74}]/X_{run\ 1,74}$

Input	Capital	Str.	Equip.	Labor	WC	Blue-Collar Unskilled	Blue-Collar Skilled
%	70.2	61.8	80.7	−26.9	−26.9	−16.5	−31.0

We can see that all capital prices rise and all labor prices fall. In addition, the price of the least skilled labor falls the least. This means that skilled labor benefits relative to unskilled labor from productivity change. Because the agricultural and miscellaneous industries are the most capital intensive, their aggregate input prices rise while the other, more labor intensive industries show falls in their aggregate input prices.

Aggregate prices, input, and output. We have previously presented in separate tables the annual average growth rates of output, input, output price and input price for the zero productivity change simulation (run 2) and the actual data (run 1) by industry. We now bring these data together for the total economy. Table 3.13 shows differences in average annual growth rates between runs 2 and 1 for the four variables listed.

Table 3.13.   Differences in Average Annual Percentage Growth Rates of Prices and Quantities of Value-Added and Aggregate Input, 1947-74

Diff.= $[Rate_{run\ 2} - Rate_{run\ 1}]$

Ind.	Q̇/Q	İ/I	Ẇ/W	Ṗ/P	Q̇/Q−İ/I=Ẇ/W−Ṗ/P
Agr.	−2.03	1.09	0.46	3.58	−3.12
Misc.	−2.85	−.56	0.21	2.50	−2.29
Const.	−4.93	−2.50	−0.65	1.79	−2.44
Mfg.	−3.44	−1.01	−0.49	1.94	−2.43
Equip.	−2.62	−0.19	−0.48	1.94	−2.42
Serv.	−3.63	−1.19	−0.65	1.78	−2.43
Total	−3.09	−0.67	−0.12	2.30	−2.42

If there had been no productivity change in any industry, agricultural output would have increased 2.03 percentage points more slowly than in the actual case, while inputs to agriculture would have increased 1.09 percentage points more quickly than in the actual case. This slower rate of growth of productivity is also shown in the faster growth of output prices relative to input prices in the alternative solution as compared to the control. We can see that lower rates of growth of productivity have their effects both in slower rates of growth of output relative to factor input and in slower rates of growth of input prices relative to output prices [as (3.14) suggests].

Functional income distribution: zero productivity change case. One of the major stimuli behind this work is the desire to say something about the effect of productivity change on the functional distribution of income. We have delineated five types of inputs: structures, equipment, white-collar labor, skilled blue-collar labor, and unskilled workers. What might we expect to find in this case? Given a 2-factor CES function such as (3.1), we can derive capital and labor input demands [(3.5) and (3.6)]. Under our assumptions, the capital and labor shares are equal to rK/Q and wL/Q, respectively. We can then derive an equation for the percentage change in labor share:

$$(3.23) \quad \dot{M}_L/M_L = [\dot{w}/w][1 - Za(s - 1)] - \dot{A}/A - (\dot{r}/r)Za(s - 1)$$
$$+ [\dot{a}][X + Z(a - s)/(1 - a)] .$$

where:

$$(3.24) \quad Z = [s/(s - 1)][AL/Q]^{(s-1)/s}[aw/(r(1 - a))]^{s-1}$$
$$X = [s/(s - 1)][AL/Q]^{(s-1)/s} ;$$

$$(3.25) \quad [M_K][\dot{M}_K/M_K] = -[M_L][\dot{M}_L/M_L].$$

From (3.23), we know that a rise in capital price will have a negative effect on labor share. This is because the elasticities of substitution which we use in this paper are less than unity (with the exception of the construction industry) which means that $-Za(s-1)$ is less than zero.

A rise in the wage rate may raise or lower labor share depending on the magnitude of $[1-Za(s-1)]$ which may be greater or less than zero. In addition, this equation suggests that technical progress will tend to reduce labor share. This effect, however, will be countered by rises in prices of inputs relative to output prices [as in (3.14)], and thus this implication of the equation cannot be accepted.

What might we expect to find as far as the effects of technical change on the relative factor shares of the three different types of labor? First, we must keep in mind what has happened in the postwar period. There has been an upgrading of the educational levels of the labor force from 1947 to 1974. Denison notes that "A sharp upward shift in the educational background of the American labor force has upgraded the skills and versatility of labor and contributed to the rise in national income ... it has also permitted a shift in occupational composition from occupations in which workers typically have little education and low earnings toward those in which education and earnings are higher."[10] Although education of the labor force rose over our time period, other changes had depressing effects on overall labor input. Rises in female employment, a large rise in part-time workers, and falls in hours worked for full-time nonfarm wage and salary workers have had negative effects on the growth rate of labor input.[11]

The major question which suggests itself when we examine labor factor shares is: Given that there has been such an expansion in the supply of skilled labor in the U.S. (labor supply is assumed exogenous in our model), why has this expansion not had more of a depressing effect on wages of skilled labor?

Gary Becker's (1964) estimates of the private rates of return to college and high school education show no declines from 1939 to 1961.[12] While since then rates of return *may* have declined, a priori one might have expected the large rise in average education to have caused declines in these rates over time if everything else were constant. Welch suggests this.[13] However, due to technical change, everything else has not been constant. Our hypothesis then is that because of technical change, labor with more skills has done better relative to labor with fewer skills. In this context, we mean that reducing technical change will hurt white-collar labor and help unskilled blue-collar labor relatively, with the effects on skilled blue-collar labor somewhere in between.

For capital inputs, we recognize that reductions in productivity growth should tend to reduce income, savings, and investment and therefore capital stock. This should tend to increase the prices of both structures and equipment, compared to the control solution. Thus we would expect that reductions in technical progress should tend to reduce the overall share of labor in the economy, given that the price of capital inputs will rise, the price of skilled labor input will fall, and that the elasticities of substitution used in the simulations are less than one (except for construction). In addition, we would expect a reduction in overall labor share in each sector with the exception of the structures sector, and industries (like agriculture) which are intensive in the use of unskilled labor. Because of the production function we assume here, in which aggregate capital and aggregate labor are Cobb-Douglas functions of the individual input types, the shares of individual factor types change in the same proportions as the overall capital and labor share, and thus they are not presented.

We can see from these tables that our hypotheses are generally supported by the simulation results. Without any productivity change, we find the share

Table 3.14. Comparison of 1974 Factor Shares by Input Type Between Run 2 and Run 1

% Diff. in End-of-Period Values=$[X_{run\ 2,74} - X_{run\ 1,74}]/X_{run\ 1,74}$

Input	Capital	Labor	Struct.	Equip.	W.C.	Blue-collar Unskilled	Skilled
Percent	23.1	-11.1	24.8	20.5	-11.8	1.8	-14.9

Table 3.15. Comparison of 1974 Overall Capital and Labor Shares by Industry Between Run 2 and Run 1

% Diff. in End-of-Period Values=$[X_{run\ 2,74} - X_{run\ 1,74}]/X_{run\ 1,74}$

Industry	Capital	Labor
Agriculture	11.5	-7.9
Miscellaneous	13.5	-11.4
Construction	-10.9	2.6
Manufacturing	19.3	-5.2
Equipment	22.7	-6.1
Services	24.0	-3.7

of skilled blue-collar and white-collar labor declining relative to the actual data. This means that the total impact of productivity change on the economy was to increase the share of white-collar and skilled blue-collar labor, and to decrease the shares of unskilled labor and capital. This is what we had expected. It indicates that without as much technical progress as actually occurred, white-collar and skilled blue-collar workers would have been worse off, and the incentives for occupational upgrading and increased skills and education would have been greatly reduced. The slight rise in the share of unskilled workers (1.8%) in the zero productivity growth run is probably attributable to the large rise in the share of agriculture in private sector GNP (from .031 to .0586, an 88% rise). This caused increases in demand for unskilled labor, which agriculture uses intensively. The strong increases in demand for inputs result from the fall in technical progress, with output not decreasing in proportion.

Because the capital share is 23.1% higher in run 2 than in run 1, we know that actual productivity change has operated to lower the capital share.

Technical progress has thus caused a 23.1% reduction in capital's share which affected structures and equipment almost equally.

Zero Productivity Change in Particular Industries

We next discuss the runs where productivity is assumed constant in only one industry and where the other industries continue to exhibit the same rates of productivity change as in the control solution. These runs are quite interesting, since they bring out the effects of simply changing one parameter. The evolution of an industry with no productivity change can thus be contrasted with industries that do exhibit increases in productivity within the same simulation.

Capital-labor ratios in production. The first important result which is evident from table 3.16 is that the overall capital stock decreases in each of the runs where one industry's rate of productivity change is held to zero. This is because of the induced accumulation effect. In run 4, where equipment increases slightly relative to the actual data, the large fall in the stock of structures reduces aggregate capital. Second, in most cases this fall in capital accumulation leads to falls in each industry's K/L ratio.

Table 3.16.   Comparison of 1974 Capital-Labor Ratios in Production
Between Run 3-7 and Run 1

% Diff. in 1974 Values=$[X_{run\ 3-7,74} - X_{run\ 1,74}]/X_{run\ 1,74}$

Industry	Run 3	Run 4	Run 5	Run 6	Run 7
Agric.	7.5	−2.6	−11.4	−22.7	6.1
Misc.	−10.9	−9.7	−8.0	−10.0	2.8
Const.	−20.6	−9.7	−6.8	−22.5	−0.4
Mfg.	−15.3	−1.7	−4.3	−21.6	0.2
Equip.	−13.9	−2.1	−4.7	−19.9	0.7
Serv.	−9.8	−4.5	−8.3	−17.8	3.6

Comparison of 1974 Structures and Equipment Stocks Between
Runs 3-7 and Run 1 (% Differences)

Structures	−9.5	−14.2	−19.3	−4.7	−5.4
Equipment	−2.3	4.1	−7.1	−29.0	−2.2

There are two exceptions to this. In run 3, the agricultural K/L ratio rises by 7.5% while all other K/L ratios decrease. This is plausible, since agriculture is intensive in the use of unskilled blue-collar labor whose relative price rises strongly. The percentage changes in input price for the five different types of inputs in this run (run 3) are given below:

| Input Type | CAPITAL | | LABOR | | |
	Struc.	Equip.	W.C.	Blue-collar Unskilled	Skilled
% Change in price (1974 Prices) (Run 3/Run 1)	4.4	12.0	-12	26	-15

Thus aggregate labor becomes more expensive in the agricultural sector, leading to substitution of capital for labor even while the capital price has risen.

The other case where capital-labor ratios rise in spite of a decrease in capital stock overall is the run where service sector productivity is held constant. It is slightly puzzling why the capital-labor ratios rise in five out of six industries when the capital stock is declining and labor input overall remains unchanged.[14] However, the explanation for this is not hard to find. Because of relative price changes, factors of production are reallocated between sectors and the size of individual sectors changes. In addition different sectors have substantially different K/L ratios, as table 3.17 shows. In this case the service sector, which has the lowest K/L ratio, increases its share of GNP at the expense of other sectors which have higher capital-labor ratios. Thus although the aggregate K/L ratio declines, five out of six of the individual sectors show rises in their K/L ratios. These two occurrences are possible because of the corresponding shifts in composition of output.[15]

Table 3.17. Output Shares and Capital-Labor Ratios by Industry, Runs 1 and 7

| Industry | Output Shares | | Capital-Labor Ratios | |
	Run 1	Run 7	Run 1	Run 7
Agric.	.0311	.0298	.798	.847
Misc.	.4797	.4361	1.494	1.536
Constr.	.0307	.0259	.362	.361
Mfg.	.2401	.2175	.368	.369
Equip.	.0754	.0730	.393	.395
Serv.	.1431	.2176	.269	.279

In the two runs (4 and 6) where Hicks-neutral productivity increases in the capital goods producing industries are held to zero, K/L ratios fall for each industry. In run 4, K/L ratios fall by 2 to 10%, while in run 6 they fall by 10 to 23%. The smaller percentage changes in run 4 are due to the smaller size of the structures-producing industry relative to the equipment-producing industry (3% versus 7.5% of private GNP in 1974, respectively) and also to the lower growth rates of productivity in structures as opposed to equipment (1.79% versus 2.0%, respectively). Run 5 also shows falls in K/L ratios in each industry. In this run, even though productivity growth in the capital goods industries is not reduced, we see substantial falls in capital accumulation because of the lower income and savings which reductions in manufacturing productivity growth cause.

Changes in capital and labor inputs. Tables 3.18, 3.19, and 3.20 show the percentage changes in units of capital, labor, and total input between the control and the alternate solutions at the end of the simulation period for the five runs under discussion. There is a very definite pattern which emerges in these runs. The industry with zero productivity growth rate increases its use of inputs strongly. For example, labor input in the affected industry increases by 35.5 to 146%, depending on the run, and capital input in the affected industry increases by between 29.6 and 165%. These increases in inputs in the one industry with no productivity growth form a strong contrast to the often dramatic reductions in inputs in the other sectors. With only three minor exceptions, the industries which experience normal productivity change show declines in their usage of inputs that are often large.[16] The increases in inputs in the affected industries result from output growth declining much less quickly than productivity growth. By simulating zero productivity growth in individual industries, we can find the direct and indirect general equilibrium effects of productivity growth. Our runs show that one major effect of productivity growth in any particular industry is to reduce drastically the inputs required in that sector. This is a variation of the effect we see in run 2, where inputs move toward those industries (construction, manufacturing, and services especially) with lower than average productivity growth and away from those industries with higher productivity growth. In runs 3-7, one industry has productivity growth much lower than average, and inputs move toward that particular industry.

Output-labor ratios. Table 3.21 shows the percentage changes in output-labor ratios between the control solution and runs 3-7, at the end of the simulation. We can see that for the five out of six industries unaffected by changes in parameters in each run, there were small declines in Q/L ratios except for run 7, where there were small rises. (3.4) is as follows:

$$(3.4) \quad \dot{Q}/Q - \dot{L}/L = \dot{A}/A + M_K[\dot{K}/K - \dot{L}/L] + [s/(a(1-a))](M_K - a)[\dot{a}].$$

Table 3.18. Comparison of 1974 Capital Inputs by Industry Between
Runs 3-7 and Run 1

% Diff. in 1974 Values = $[X_{run\ 3-7,74} - X_{run\ 1,74}]/X_{run\ 1,74}$

Industry	Run 3	Run 4	Run 5	Run 6	Run 7
Agric.	+ 165.	−6.1	−24.3	−22.5	−5.1
Misc.	−14.0	−9.2	−19.6	−13.7	−8.6
Constr.	−36.6	+ 43.7	−12.8	−54.2	−14.9
Mfg.	−21.0	−5.3	+ 29.6	−26.0	−9.3
Equip.	−12.2	−13.1	−25.0	+ 33.3	−3.1
Serv.	−16.8	−7.7	−22.7	−23.5	+ 50.8

Table 3.19. Comparison of 1974 Labor Inputs by Industry Between
Runs 3-7 and Run 1

% Diff. in 1974 Values = $[X_{run\ 3-7,74} - X_{run\ 1,74}]/X_{run\ 1,74}$

Industry	Run 3	Run 4	Run 5	Run 6	Run 7
Agric.	+ 146.7	−3.5	−14.6	++ 0.3	−10.5
Misc.	−3.5	++ 0.5	−12.6	−4.1	−11.2
Constr.	−20.2	+ 59.1	−6.5	−40.9	−14.6
Mfg.	−6.8	−3.7	+ 35.5	−5.7	−9.4
Equip.	++ 1.9	−11.2	−21.3	+ 66.4	−3.8
Serv.	−7.7	−3.3	−15.7	−6.8	+ 45.5

+ Industry affected by zero productivity change assumption.
++ Percent changes greater than zero in an industry with unchanged rates of productivity growth.

The third term is negligible, and $\dot{A}/A$ does not vary for five out of six of the industries. Thus for the industries with unchanged productivity parameters, the main determinant of the change in the Q/L ratio is the change in the K/L ratio. We see that for those industries, the signs and magnitudes of the K/L and Q/L changes match quite well. For the one industry in each run where productivity change is held to zero, the major determinant of the fall in Q/L, or labor productivity, is the reduction in the rate of growth of total factor productivity.

The magnitude of the falls in Q/L compare with the magnitude of falls in productivity growth, with agriculture showing the largest and construction the smallest reduction in both Q/L and $\dot{A}/A$.

Table 3.20. Comparison of 1974 Total Input by Industry Between Runs 3-7 and Run 1

% Diff. in 1974 Values=$[X_{run\ 3-7,74}-X_{run\ 1,74}]/X_{run\ 1,74}$

Industry	Run 3	Run 4	Run 5	Run 6	Run 7
Agric.	+ 153.7	-4.6	-18.8	-10.0	-8.4
Misc.	-8.0	-4.1	-15.9	-8.7	-10.1
Constr.	-23.7	+ 56.1	-7.7	-43.6	-14.6
Manuf.	-9.9	-4.1	+ 34.2	-10.6	-9.4
Equip.	-1.1	-11.6	-22.1	+ 58.4	-3.6
Serv.	-8.9	-3.9	-16.7	-9.3	+ 46.1

+ Industry affected by zero productivity growth assumption.

Table 3.21. Comparison of 1974 Output-Labor Ratios Between Runs 3-7 and Run 1

% Diff. in 1974 Values = $[X_{run\ 1,74}-X_{run\ 3-7,74}]/X_{run\ 1,74}$

Industry	Run 3	Run 4	Run 5	Run 6	Run 7
Agric.	+ -65.2	-1.1	-4.8	-10.2	2.4
Misc.	-5.2	-4.6	-3.8	-4.8	1.3
Constr.	-4.2	+ -39.5	-1.3	-4.7	-0.1
Mfg.	-3.5	-0.4	+ -41.2	-5.2	0.0
Equip.	-3.2	-0.5	-1.0	+ -44.5	0.1
Serv.	-1.4	-0.6	-1.2	-2.7	+ -41.9

+ Industry affected by zero productivity change assumption.

Total output and intermediate input. Tables 3.22, 3.23, and 3.24 present the growth rates of gross output, intermediate input, and value-added for the control run and the five industry productivity runs.

Tables 3.25, 3.26, and 3.27 show percentage differences in growth rates for gross output, intermediate input, and value-added between run 1 and runs 3-7. For each run, the growth rates of total output are weighted averages of the growth rates of intermediate input and value-added.

Table 3.22.   Average Annual Percentage Growth Rates of Gross Output, 1947-74, for Runs 3-7 and Run 1 by Industry

				Rates = $\mathrm{Log}[X_{74}/X_{47}]/27$			
Industry	Ctrl.	Run 3	Run 4	Run 5	Run 6	Run 7
Agric.	2.10	1.53 +	1.92	1.33	1.71	1.77
Misc.	3.83	3.50	3.67	3.18	3.49	3.44
Constr.	2.74	1.75	2.60 +	2.44	0.62	2.16
Manuf.	3.13	2.74	2.98	2.29 +	2.71	2.77
Equip.	3.33	3.34	2.88	2.41	3.04 +	3.20
Serv.	3.64	3.29	3.40	2.97	3.28	3.02 +

Table 3.23.   Average Annual Percentage Growth Rates of Intermediate Input, 1947-74, for Runs 3-7 and Run 1 by Industry

				Rates = $\mathrm{Log}[X_{74}/X_{47}]/27$			
Industry	Ctrl.	Run 3	Run 4	Run 5	Run 6	Run 7
Agric.	2.72	0.98 +	2.59	2.14	2.32	2.45
Misc.	3.87	3.67	3.68	3.43	3.60	3.82
Constr.	2.59	1.75	1.77 +	2.52	0.59	2.15
Manuf.	2.93	2.82	2.82	1.57 +	2.62	2.71
Equip.	3.09	3.34	2.68	2.48	1.93 +	3.10
Serv.	4.08	3.85	4.01	3.75	3.87	2.44 +

+ Industry affected by zero productivity change assumption.

Table 3.24.   Average Annual Percentage Growth Rates of Value-Added, 1947-74, for Runs 3-7 and Run 1 by Industry

$$\text{Rates} = \text{Log}[X_{74}/X_{47}]/27$$

Industry	Ctrl.	Run 3	Run 4	Run 5	Run 6	Run 7
Agric.	1.15	2.11 +	0.90	0.0	0.78	0.73
Misc.	3.81	3.41	3.67	3.07	3.44	3.25
Constr.	3.05	1.75	3.98 +	2.27	0.69	2.17
Manuf.	3.45	2.59	3.25	3.29 +	2.89	2.87
Equip.	3.67	3.20	3.16	2.30	4.25 +	3.33
Serv.	3.32	2.87	4.21	2.33	2.83	3.36 +

Table 3.25.   Percentage Differences in Average Annual Growth Rates of Gross Output Between Runs 3-7 and Run 1 by Industry

$$\% \text{ Differences} = [\text{Rate}_{\text{run } 3-7} - \text{Rate}_{\text{run } 1}]/\text{Rate}_{\text{run } 1}$$

Industry	Run 3	Run 4	Run 5	Run 6	Run 7
Agric.	-27.2 +	-8.3	-36.7	-18.5	-15.4
Misc.	-8.6	-4.1	-16.8	-8.8	-10.2
Constr.	-36.3	-5.0 +	-10.9	-77.5	-21.4
Manuf.	-12.6	-4.9	-26.9 +	-13.2	-11.7
Equip.	-1.5	-13.7	-27.8	-8.8 +	-4.1
Serv.	-9.6	-4.1	-18.6	-10.0	-17.1 +

+ Industry affected by zero productivity growth assumption.

A clear pattern seems to be visible as far as the changes in value-added and intermediate input are concerned. In runs 3-7, the industry affected by the zero productivity change assumption has value-added growth rates that increase *most* or decrease *least* of all the industries in that run. However, the affected industry also has growth rates of intermediate input which decrease *most* or increase *least*.[17] This is what we might expect. As Hulten (1979) points out,

Table 3.26. Percentage Differences in Average Annual Growth Rates of Intermediate Input Between Runs 3-7 and Run 1

% Differences = $[\text{Rate}_{\text{run } 3\text{-}7} - \text{Rate}_{\text{run } 1}]/\text{Rate}_{\text{run } 1}$

Industry	Run 3	Run 4	Run 5	Run 6	Run 7
Agric.	+ −64.1	−4.9	−21.5	−14.6	−10.1
Misc.	−5.1	−4.9	−11.4	−6.8	−1.1
Constr.	−32.7	+ −31.6	−2.9	−77.4	−17.2
Manuf.	−4.0	−4.0	+ −46.5	−10.9	−7.8
Equip.	7.9	−13.5	−19.9	+ −37.6	0.4
Serv.	−5.5	−1.6	−7.9	−5.2	+ −40.6

Table 3.27. Percentage Differences in Average Annual Growth Rates of Value-Added Between Runs 3-7 and Run 1

% Differences = $[\text{Rate}_{\text{run } 3\text{-}7} - \text{Rate}_{\text{run } 1}]/\text{Rate}_{\text{run } 1}$

Industry	Run 3	Run 4	Run 5	Run 6	Run 7
Agric.	+ 83.3	−21.8	−99.7	−32.2	−36.4
Misc.	−10.3	−3.7	−19.6	−9.7	−14.8
Constr.	−42.7	+ 30.3	−25.6	−77.4	−28.8
Manuf.	−24.9	−6.1	+ −4.9	−16.3	−17.0
Equip.	−12.6	−13.9	−37.2	+ 16.0	−9.2
Serv.	−13.7	−6.6	−30.0	−14.9	+ 1.2

+ Industry affected by zero productivity growth assumption.

increases in productivity affect intermediate input, which then serves to magnify the effects of technical change. Since we are reducing the growth of productivity in these runs, we should expect to see this effect working in reverse. In other words, increases in productivity growth in one sector increase intermediate input and total output in other sectors. We have here another indication that the total effect of productivity change is greater than the direct effect in any one industry. Thus our main conclusion is that increases in productivity in any one industry will cause the growth of total output and intermediate input in other industries to be more than it would have been otherwise.

The fact that value-added growth rates of the affected industries increase most when compared to the actual data can be put down to the fact that productivity decreases more than output does. This forces increases in employment of inputs and a consequent rise in value-added.

Producer prices and input prices. If we examine the percentage changes in producer prices, a clear pattern develops. The industry affected by low productivity growth exhibits large rises in its output prices. Depending on the size of the industry, other industries are also affected. Thus zero productivity growth in manufacturing affects other industries' prices more than the same assumption applied to agriculture.

Another conclusion can be drawn, and that is that the price of capital to industry rises in all of these cases except run 7. We can see this another way by

Table 3.28.   Comparison of 1974 Producer Goods Prices by Industry Between Runs 3-7 and Run 1

% Diff. in 1974 Values=$[X_{run\ 3-7,74} - X_{run\ 1,74}]/X_{run\ 1,74}$					
Industry	Run 3	Run 4	Run 5	Run 6	Run 7
Agric.	+ 129.2	0.2	7.3	5.5	6.2
Misc.	-1.0	3.9	5.4	0.5	4.7
Constr.	-0.1	+ 21.7	17.5	3.6	6.0
Manuf.	5.0	0.2	+ 43.0	4.2	5.0
Equip.	4.1	0.1	13.9	+ 35.1	4.9
Serv.	-1.2	-0.1	5.2	-0.2	+ 48.8
Output share of affected industry	.031	.031	.240	.075	.143
% rise in overall Consumption goods prices	2.5	2.0	17.1	1.6	11.8

+   Industry affected by zero productivity growth assumption.

examining the percentage changes in the economy-wide price of each input type (table 3.32). In all runs except run 7, the capital price is higher and the labor price is lower with lower productivity change. Thus we can see that productivity change in each of these industries except services actually hurt owners of capital. Productivity change in services actually helped owners of capital because of the labor intensity of this industry.

Table 3.29. Percentage Differences in Average Annual Growth Rates of Capital Input Price Between Runs 3-7 and Run 1 by Industry [++]

$$\% \text{ Differences} = [\text{Rate}_{\text{run } 3\text{-}7} - \text{Rate}_{\text{run } 1}]/\text{Rate}_{\text{run } 1}$$

Industry	Run 3	Run 4	Run 5	Run 6	Run 7
Agric.	47.4 [+]	0.9	31.0	125.1	−6.0
Misc.	171.7	336.4	251.0	213.4	−62.9
Constr.	35.1	33.5 [+]	36.6	68.8	−8.3
Manuf.	82.1	4.1	54.8 [+]	215.2	−10.7
Equip.	68.3	7.6	47.4	176.1 [+]	−9.5
Serv.	32.4	13.9	26.7	75.9	−5.8 [+]

Table 3.30. Percentage Differences in Average Annual Growth Rates of Labor Input Price Between Runs 3-7 and Run 1 by Industry

$$\% \text{ Differences} = [\text{Rate}_{\text{run } 3\text{-}7} - \text{Rate}_{\text{run } 1}]/\text{Rate}_{\text{run } 1}$$

Industry	Run 3	Run 4	Run 5	Run 6	Run 7
Agric.	21.0 [+]	−3.6	−10.5	−9.2	7.2
Misc.	−14.9	−3.6	−4.2	−10.7	2.5
Constr.	−20.8	−2.6 [+]	3.3	−11.9	−3.6
Manuf.	−17.3	−2.5	−0.8 [+]	−9.8	−1.4
Equip.	−16.3	−2.7	−0.4	−9.9 [+]	−0.5
Serv.	−11.0	−5.2	−9.4	−13.9	6.3 [+]

+ Industry affected by zero productivity change assumption.
++ Overall capital and labor input prices vary by industry because the industries vary in the composition of capital and labor from the individual input types. See (3.15) and (3.16), p. 70.

Table 3.31. Percentage Differences in Average Annual Growth Rates of Aggregate Input Price Between Runs 3-7 and Run 1 by Industry

% Differences = [Rate$_{run\ 3-7}$- Rate$_{run\ 1}$]/Rate$_{run\ 1}$

Industry	Run 3	Run 4	Run 5	Run 6	Run 7
Agric.	20.6 +	-2.6	-4.3	7.3	4.7
Misc.	-8.4	9.5	5.5	-2.5	0.2
Constr.	-16.8	0.5 +	6.3	-5.4	-4.2
Manuf.	-13.8	-2.3	3.1 +	-0.4	-1.9
Equip.	-12.6	-2.3	1.9	-0.9 +	-1.0
Serv.	-9.9	-4.8	-8.5	-9.5	6.7 +

+   Industry affected by zero productivity growth assumption.

Table 3.32. Comparison of 1974 Values of Input Prices by Type of Input Between Runs 3-7 and Run 1

% Diff. in 1974 Values = [X$_{run\ 3-7}$-X$_{run\ 1}$]/X$_{run\ 1}$

Input Type	Run 3	Run 4	Run 5	Run 6	Run 7
White-Collar Labor	-12.24	-3.02	-5.41	-7.28	4.01
Unskilled Blue-Collar	26.11	-3.40	-9.97	-8.22	7.45
Skilled Blue-Collar	-15.18	-0.62	6.73	-6.37	-5.61
Overall Labor	-8.07	-2.28	-2.03	-7.11	1.31
Structures	4.40	19.66	10.80	-1.50	-2.70
Equipment	11.99	-4.62	5.51	39.79	-0.83
Overall Capital	9.64	2.89	7.14	27.01	-1.87

Two other conclusions can be drawn from runs 3 and 5. In these runs, while the overall labor price fell, one individual labor type (unskilled blue-collar and skilled blue-collar respectively) benefited from a rise in its price. This means that agricultural productivity change tended to reduce incomes of unskilled labor, and manufacturing productivity change tended to reduce the income of skilled blue-collar workers.

Functional distribution of income. We have touched on the functional distribution of income in examining the changes in input prices between the control and alternate solutions. Let us now examine the changes in factor shares for each input type, overall and by industry. The data are presented in tables 3.33, 3.34, and 3.35.

Table 3.33. Comparison of 1974 Factor Shares by Input Type Between Runs 3-7 and Run 1 for the Total Economy

% Differences in 1974 Values $=[X_{\text{run } 3\text{-}7,74} - X_{\text{run } 1,74}]/X_{\text{run } 1,74}$

Input Type	Run 3	Run 4	Run 5	Run 6	Run 7
Structures	0.25	3.7	-6.5	0.3	-7.3
Equipment	12.3	0.35	4.3	6.7	-3.5
Overall Capital	5.2	2.3	-2.1	2.9	-5.7
White-Collar Labor	-7.2	-1.9	-2.9	-1.8	5.8
Unskilled Blue-Collar	35.9	-2.2	-8.1	-3.0	10.2
Skilled Blue-Collar	-9.6	0.6	10.7	-0.2	-5.0
Overall Labor	-2.5	-1.1	1.0	-1.4	2.8

Several conclusions are evident from these tables. Looking first at the changes in shares by industry, we can see that our assumptions on elasticities of substitution are important. The construction industry is the only one in our model with an elasticity of substitution greater than unity, and with one exception, it is the only industry where capital share falls and labor share rises in runs 3-6. All the other industries show rising capital shares and falling labor shares in runs 3-6 resulting from rising capital prices. The one exception is agriculture in run 3. In this case, capital share falls in spite of rising capital prices. The reason for this is the rise in the price of unskilled labor in which agriculture is intensive, causing labor to become more expensive in agriculture but less expensive elsewhere.

Turning to economy-wide changes in factor shares, certain conclusions carry over from our examination of changes in input prices. Agricultural productivity change hurt capital and unskilled labor relative to skilled labor, ceteris paribus. For run 5, manufacturing productivity change reduced the

Table 3.34.   Comparison of 1974 Capital Shares by Industry Between
Runs 3-7 and Run 1

% Differences in 1974 Values $=[X_{run\ 3-7,74}-X_{run\ 1,74}]/X_{run\ 1,74}$

Industry	Run 3	Run 4	Run 5	Run 6	Run 7
Agric.	+(-1.43)	0.52	2.40	5.15	-1.16
Misc.	2.68	2.36	1.93	2.44	-0.65
Constr.	-2.59	+(-1.14)	-0.79	-2.82	-0.04
Manuf.	4.54	0.46	+1.19	6.69	-0.04
Equip.	5.14	0.71	1.63	+7.70	-0.23
Serv.	3.91	1.73	3.27	7.53	+(-1.31)

+ Industry affected by zero productivity growth assumption.

Table 3.35.   Comparison of 1974 Labor Shares by Industry Between
Runs 3-7 and Run 1

% Diff. in 1974 Values $= [X_{run\ 3-7,74}-X_{run\ 1,74}]/X_{run\ 1,74}$

Industry	Run 3	Run 4	Run 5	Run 6	Run 7
Agric.	+0.97	-0.36	-1.64	-3.52	0.80
Misc.	-2.28	-2.00	-1.64	-2.08	0.55
Constr.	0.61	+0.27	0.19	0.66	0.01
Manuf.	-1.22	-0.12	+(-0.32)	-1.80	0.01
Equip.	-1.39	-0.19	-0.44	+(-2.08)	0.06
Serv.	-0.60	-0.27	-0.50	-1.16	+0.20

+ Industry affected by zero productivity growth assumption.

share of skilled blue-collar workers, but raised that of capital as a whole. This
occurred in spite of increased capital stock and reduced capital prices relative
to the control solution, and because of the intensity of manufacturing in skilled
blue-collar labor. Therefore the effect of manufacturing productivity change
was to reduce the earnings of skilled blue-collar labor. Productivity change in

services reduced the share of labor and increased the share of capital. Productivity change in the service sector only hurt white-collar workers relative to capital, while productivity change in the other sectors helped white-collar workers.

Alternative Assumptions on Overall Productivity Growth

We now examine the effects in our model of changing assumptions about every industry's rate of productivity growth in each run. These runs (runs 8-11) differ from those in the previous section because we change the rate of growth of productivity in each industry, rather than just in one industry. Thus they have some similarities to run 2, where every industry's productivity growth was eliminated. The runs examined here are:

(a) Run 8—Each industry is given the average growth rate or productivity for the whole period 1947-74.

(b) Run 9—Each industry has 1/2 the average rate for the period.

(c) Run 10—Productivity change in each industry is held to zero after 1965, thus aggravating the productivity slowdown.

(d) Run 11—Each industry is given the 1947-65 rate of productivity growth in the 1965-74 period. Thus in this run there is no productivity slowdown.

K/L and Q/L ratios and units of input. The major conclusion which we can draw from runs 8-11 can be seen by comparing the differences in rates of total factor productivity growth (table 3.41) with the percentage changes in aggregate input, capital, and labor between runs 8-11 and run 1, the actual situation. In these cases, for any sector the higher (the more positive) the percentage point difference between the run 1 and alternative solution productivity growth, the more that inputs tend to be reallocated toward that sector. For example, in run 11, the service sector has the highest (least negative) percentage point difference in productivity growth between the control and the alternate assumption, and it has the largest increase in *K*, *L*, and total input overall. For runs 8 and 9, agricultural capital, labor, and input increase most (or decrease least) because agricultural productivity growth decreases substantially while demand for agricultural output does not.[18]

What these results indicate is that inputs in our runs tend to move toward the industries (agriculture, miscellaneous, and equipment) with higher than average technical change in the control run. In other words, the actual U.S. growth process caused factors to move out of those industries into others (construction, manufacturing, and especially services) with lower productivity growth in actuality.

We can see the effects of changes in productivity growth rates on K/L ratios in table 3.36. The fact that K/L ratios fall for all industries in run 8 is at first glance puzzling. In this run, as table 3.41 shows, all industries except agriculture increased their rates of productivity growth. Both the construction and equipment-producing industries showed greater productivity increases than in the control solution. One would expect this to lead to great capital accumulation. However, this is not the case. The K/L ratios are lower than in the control solution in all industries, and there is a smaller capital stock. In addition, the relative prices of capital goods rise and those of labor fall, leading to substitution away from labor to capital. Since labor input is exogeneous to this model, changes in the aggregate K/L ratio are due to capital only.

Table 3.36.   Comparison of 1974 Capital-Labor Ratios by Industry
Between Runs 8-11 and Run 1

% Diff. in 1974 Values = $[X_{run\ 8-11,74} - X_{run\ 1,74}]/X_{run\ 1,74}$

Industry	Run 8	Run 9	Run 10	Run 11
Agric.	-8.2	-30.4	-2.1	10.2
Misc.	-9.0	-29.0	-3.8	6.6
Constr.	-14.5	-44.2	-7.8	11.5
Manuf.	-10.0	-32.0	-4.9	9.3
Equip.	-9.4	-30.3	-4.4	8.7
Serv.	-9.2	-29.7	-3.3	8.9

Table 3.37.   Comparison of 1974 Output-Labor Ratios by Industry
Between Runs 8-11 and Run 1

% Diff. in 1974 Values = $[X_{run\ 8-11,74} - X_{run\ 1,74}]/X_{run\ 1,74}$

Industry	Run 8	Run 9	Run 10	Run 11
Agric.	-17.7	-47.5	-11.5	50.8
Misc.	1.5	-35.5	-5.4	32.3
Constr.	7.7	-28.6	-10.4	12.7
Manuf.	3.9	-30.1	3.5	41.4
Equip.	2.0	-31.2	0.4	36.0
Serv.	21.6	-16.0	-8.9	16.6

Table 3.38. Comparison of 1974 Capital Input Overall and by Industry Between Runs 8-11 and Run 1

% Diff. in 1974 Values = $[X_{run\ 8-11} - X_{run\ 1}]/X_{run\ 1}$

Industry	Run 8	Run 9	Run 10	Run 11
Agric.	14.9	-9.5	7.6	-2.0
Misc.	-6.5	-24.7	-2.4	5.5
Constr.	-20.3	-52.8	-20.7	10.0
Manuf.	-9.7	-33.5	-11.1	2.5
Equip.	-5.4	-25.1	2.6	13.6
Serv.	-20.6	-43.5	0.9	22.8
Structure stock	-6.6	-24.9	-2.5	3.8
Equipment stock	-7.9	-29.9	-3.3	10.6

Table 3.39. Comparison of 1974 Labor Input by Industry Between Runs 8-11 and Run 1

% Diff. in 1974 Values = $[X_{run\ 8-11} - X_{run\ 1}]/X_{run\ 1}$

Industry	Run 8	Run 9	Run 10	Run 11
Agric.	25.1	29.9	9.9	-11.1
Misc.	2.7	6.1	1.4	-1.0
Constr.	-6.8	-15.5	-14.1	-1.3
Manuf.	0.4	-2.2	-6.5	-6.3
Equip.	4.5	7.4	7.3	-4.5
Serv.	-12.5	-19.6	4.4	12.8

It appears that in this simulation, although the rates of productivity change in the structures and equipment-producing industries rise slightly, they do not increase as much as the rate of productivity growth in the service industries. This rise in service sector productivity, combined with rises in productivity of other consumption goods industries, leads to a fall in the relative prices of consumption goods.[19] This fall leads to a rise in real personal consumption expenditure of about 4%, and thus to lower capital accumulation.[20] In addition, in this run the structures industry shows a decrease in growth of value-added in spite of the higher productivity change.

Table 3.40. Comparison of 1974 Total Input by Industry Between
Runs 8-11 and Run 1

% Differences in 1974 Values=$[X_{run\ 8-11,74}-X_{run\ 1,74}]/X_{run\ 1,74}$

Industry	Run 8	Run 9	Run 10	Run 11
Agric.	21.0	12.1	9.0	-7.7
Misc.	-1.2	-8.3	-0.1	1.5
Constr.	-9.6	-24.8	-15.4	0.8
Manuf.	-1.8	-9.9	-7.5	-4.6
Equip.	2.4	-0.4	6.4	6.2
Serv.	-13.6	-23.1	4.0	13.9

Table 3.41. Average Annual Percentage Changes in Total Factor
Productivity (Value-Added Base), and Differences from Actual Growth

Rates = $Log[X_{74}/X_{47}]/27$ Differences = $[Rate_{run\ 1}-Rate_{run\ 8-11}]$

Ind.	Run 1	Run 8 Rate	Diff.	Run 9 Rate	Diff.	Run 10 Rate	Diff.	Run 11 Rate	Diff.
Agr.	3.07	2.52	.56	1.26	1.82	3.01	.06	4.52	-1.45
Misc	2.27	2.52	-.25	1.26	1.01	2.11	.15	3.17	-.91
Cons	2.10	2.52	-.42	1.26	.84	1.91	.19	2.86	-.76
Mfg.	2.26	2.52	-.26	1.26	1.00	2.12	.13	3.18	-.93
Eq.	2.33	2.52	-.19	1.26	1.07	2.14	.19	3.22	-.89
Serv	1.71	2.52	-.81	1.26	.81	1.60	.11	2.40	-.69

Gross output, intermediate input, and value-added. In runs 8-11, the growth rates of value-added, intermediate input, and gross output conform to the assumptions on productivity change. Growth rates in run 9 are substantially below, and those in run 11 substantially above the control because of total factor productivity growth rates that follow the same pattern (see table 3.42). Growth rates in runs 8 and 10 are generally closer to the control growth rates because of less substantial changes in productivity growth rates.

Producer prices. Producer prices in runs 8-11 tend to move in the opposite direction from rates of productivity growth in table 3.41. For example, in run 8, the only industry showing a fall in productivity growth (agriculture) is the only one to show a rise in productivity relative to the actual situation. In runs 9 and 10, productivity grows less quickly than in run 1, while producer prices grow more quickly. In run 11 the opposite is true. Consumer prices tend to move in the same direction as producer prices.

Input prices and share changes. As we can see by examining the changes in factor shares and factor prices in tables 3.44-3.48, reductions in the overall rate of productivity growth (runs 9 and 10) tend to raise capital's price and share of income relative to labor. On the other hand, increases in productivity growth (run 11) reduce capital prices and shares relative to labor. In addition, in our model, reductions in the dispersion of output growth rates with no reduction in overall productivity growth tend to reduce labor share. This means that, in actuality, productivity change has tended to reduce the share of capital and its price. Input prices broken down by industry (tables 3.44-3.46) tend to follow the same pattern. In runs 8-11 if the capital price increases more quickly than in the control solution, the price of labor increases less quickly. Also, in runs 8-10 the unskilled labor shares and prices increase more (or decrease less) than the shares and prices of the more skilled labor types. This suggests that reductions in technical progress (as in runs 9 and 10) or even changes in the pattern of technical progress with no aggregate reduction (run 8) would have benefited unskilled labor relative to skilled labor, and therefore that actual technical progress has helped skilled labor relative to unskilled labor and to capital. A major reason for this is the intensiveness of agriculture in unskilled labor. When agriculture experienced large productivity increases, demand for unskilled labor decreased, its price was affected, and skilled labor benefited relatively. Readjusting the pattern of technical progress away from agriculture toward other industries less intensive in the use of unskilled labor as we do in runs 8-10 reverses this pattern.

Table 3.42. Average Annual Growth Rates of Gross Output,
Intermediate Input, and Value-Added for Runs 8-11, and
Differences from Run 1

Growth Rates=Log$[X_{74}/X_{47}]$/27 | Differences=Rate$_{run\ 1}$-Rate$_{run\ 8-11}$

GROSS OUTPUT

Ind.	Run 1	Run 8 Rate	Diff.	Run 9 Rate	Diff.	Run 10 Rate	Diff.	Run 11 Rate	Diff.
Agr.	2.10	2.21	-.11	0.68	1.42	1.99	.10	3.18	-1.09
Misc	3.83	3.98	-.16	2.42	1.40	3.67	.16	4.82	-1.00
Cons	2.74	2.76	-.01	0.87	1.87	1.77	.97	3.14	-.39
Mfg.	3.13	3.29	-.16	1.72	1.41	3.01	.12	4.18	-1.04
Eq.	3.33	3.57	-.24	2.22	1.12	3.61	-.28	4.64	-1.30
Serv	3.64	3.87	-.23	2.19	1.45	3.46	.19	4.65	-1.01

INTERMEDIATE INPUT

Ind.	Run 1	Run 8 Rate	Diff.	Run 9 Rate	Diff.	Run 10 Rate	Diff.	Run 11 Rate	Diff.
Agr.	2.72	2.58	.14	1.02	1.70	2.51	.21	3.93	-1.21
Misc	3.87	3.93	-.07	2.28	1.59	3.70	.17	4.91	-1.04
Cons	2.59	2.67	-.08	0.85	1.74	1.54	1.05	2.76	-.17
Mfg.	2.93	3.12	-.18	1.61	1.33	2.92	.02	4.06	-1.12
Eq.	3.09	3.32	-.23	2.03	1.06	3.44	-.35	4.42	-1.33
Serv	4.08	4.61	-.54	3.07	1.01	3.78	.30	4.82	-.74

VALUE-ADDED

Ind.	Run 1	Run 8 Rate	Diff.	Run 9 Rate	Diff.	Run 10 Rate	Diff.	Run 11 Rate	Diff.
Agr.	1.15	1.68	-.53	0.20	.95	1.24	-.09	2.00	-.85
Misc	3.81	4.00	-.20	2.49	1.32	3.66	.15	4.78	-.98
Cons	3.05	2.94	.11	0.91	2.14	2.24	.82	3.86	-.80
Mfg.	3.46	3.57	-.11	1.91	1.54	3.16	.30	4.38	-.92
Eq.	3.67	3.91	-.24	2.47	1.19	3.85	-.19	4.94	-1.27
Serv	3.32	3.27	.05	1.46	1.87	3.23	.10	4.54	-1.22

Table 3.43. Comparison of 1974 Producer and Consumer Prices by Industry Between Runs 8-11 and Run 1

% Differences = $[X_{\text{run }8\text{-}11,74}-X_{\text{run }1,74}]/X_{\text{run }1,74}$				
Industry	Run 8	Run 9	Run 10	Run 11
Agric.	7.8	54.9	8.9	-27.9
Misc.	-5.2	37.8	4.6	-22.5
Constr.	-8.3	25.7	3.7	-18.8
Mfg.	-6.2	29.2	-1.1	-25.6
Equip.	-5.5	30.0	0.0	-24.5
Serv.	-14.7	15.9	6.4	-16.3
Overall Consumer Prices	-7.0	31.6	3.1	-22.5

Table 3.44. Average Annual Growth Rates of Prices of Capital by Industry and Differences Between Runs 8-11 and Run 1

Growth Rates=$\text{Log}[X_{74}/X_{47}]/27$		Differences=$\text{Rate}_{\text{run }1}-\text{Rate}_{\text{run }8\text{-}11}$							
		Run 8		Run 9		Run 10		Run 11	
Ind.	Run 1	Rate	Diff.	Rate	Diff.	Rate	Diff.	Rate	Diff.
Agr	.77	1.13	-.36	2.07	-1.30	.92	-.15	.41	.36
Misc	.13	.46	-.33	1.33	-1.20	.27	-.14	-.09	.22
Cons	.81	1.15	-.34	2.05	-1.24	.95	-.15	.53	.27
Mfg.	.44	.80	-.36	1.74	-1.30	.57	-.13	.08	.35
Eq.	.52	.87	-.36	1.81	-1.29	.66	-.15	.17	.35
Serv	1.00	1.35	-.35	2.27	-1.27	1.14	-.15	.68	.32

Table 3.45. Average Annual Growth Rates of Prices of Labor by
Industry and Differences Between Runs 8-11 and Run 1

Growth Rates=Log$[X_{74}/X_{47}]/27$					Differences=Rate$_{run\ 8-11}$-Rate$_{run\ 1}$			
		Run 8		Run 9		Run 10		Run 11
Ind.	Run 1	Rate	Diff.	Rate	Diff.	Rate	Diff.	Rate	Diff.
Agr	3.42	3.36	.06	2.93	.49	3.46	-.04	3.54	-.12
Misc	2.58	2.41	.17	1.97	.61	2.52	.06	2.70	-.12
Cons	2.17	2.02	.16	1.56	.61	2.06	.11	2.25	-.07
Mfg.	2.69	2.52	.16	2.07	.62	2.59	.10	2.78	-.09
Eq.	2.70	2.53	.17	2.08	.62	2.61	.09	2.79	-.10
Serv	2.04	1.88	.16	1.45	.59	2.01	.03	2.18	-.13

Table 3.46. Average Annual Growth Rates of Total Input Price by
Industry and Differences Between Runs 8-11 and Run 1

Growth Rates=Log$[X_{74}/X_{47}]/27$					Differences=Rate$_{run\ 8-11}$-Rate$_{run\ 1}$			
		Run 8		Run 9		Run 10		Run 11
Ind.	Run 1	Rate	Diff.	Rate	Diff.	Rate	Diff.	Rate	Diff.
Agr	2.81	2.92	-.11	2.28	.53	2.89	-.09	2.74	.07
Misc	1.45	1.49	-.04	1.63	-.19	1.47	-.02	1.43	.02
Cons	1.83	1.77	.06	1.57	.25	1.77	.06	1.83	.00
Mfg.	2.11	2.06	.06	1.91	.20	2.06	.05	2.11	.00
Eq.	2.18	2.12	.06	1.97	.20	2.13	.04	2.18	-.01
Serv	1.58	1.48	.10	1.23	.35	1.57	.01	1.66	-.08

Predicting with Our Model

The final simulation which we undertook was a simulation beginning in 1972 and running through 1978. The purpose of this was to check the ability of our model to track the actual course of the U.S. economy, which was perturbed by the energy crisis and a recession which occurred in 1974-75. If our model is able

Table 3.47. Percentage Changes in End-of-Period Input Price and
Factor Shares by Type of Input (Runs 8-11/Run 1)

Input	Run 8 Price	Share	Run 9 Price	Share	Run 10 Price	Share	Run 11 Price	Share
Structures	8.7	4.3	55.9	14.1	3.8	2.1	−3.9	−2.3
Equipment	10.7	4.4	36.5	11.8	4.2	1.1	·10.6	−3.4
WC labor	−5.1	−3.1	−15.5	−7.2	−1.0	0.0	4.2	2.7
Unskilled BC labor	−1.2	0.9	−11.9	−3.2	1.6	2.8	3.3	1.9
Skilled BC labor	−4.1	−1.5	−15.7	−6.1	−4.3	−3.4	1.0	−1.1
Total Capital	9.6	4.3	39.7	13.2	4.0	1.7	−6.9	−2.8
Total Labor	−4.3	−2.1	−15.1	−6.3	−1.8	−0.8	3.0	1.3

Table 3.48. Percentage Change in End-of-Period Capital and Labor
Shares by Industry (Runs 8-11/Run 1)

Industry	Run 8 K	L	Run 9 K	L	Run 10 K	L	Run 11 K	L
Agric.	1.7	−1.2	7.2	−4.9	0.4	−0.3	−1.9	1.3
Misc.	2.2	−1.9	8.0	−6.8	0.9	−0.8	−1.5	1.3
Constr.	−1.7	0.4	−6.4	1.5	−0.9	0.2	1.2	−0.3
Manuf.	2.9	−0.8	10.8	−2.9	1.3	−0.4	−2.4	0.6
Equip.	3.4	−0.9	12.7	−3.4	1.5	−0.4	−2.8	0.8
Serv.	3.6	−0.6	13.8	−2.1	1.3	−0.2	−3.1	0.5

to track the movements of the actual economy outside of the sample period, then we will have more confidence in it. We should note that our model cannot generate a business cycle so that the actual business cycle will not be exactly tracked by our simulation results. We hope, however, that as the U.S. economy recovers from the recession in 1976 and later years, the simulation results will come closer to the actual situation.

We used the following procedure in order to generate this run. Because the run began in 1972, we take the production and demand parameters for that year (except for the productivity growth rates) and use them for the whole simulation. This is one possible source of inaccuracy in this run. The 1972 parameters are derived in such a way that they can generate the 1972 data when used in a simulation. However, without changes, the parameters may diverge further and further from the true ones as time goes by. If the model is still able to predict within a reasonable degree of accuracy even with this source of error, our confidence in it should be increased.

We did not begin our projection run in 1947 for the following reasons. Our model, because of the way in which its parameters were chosen, is able to exactly reproduce the data for each individual year, such as 1947, 1958, etc. This is because we alter the parameters every year so that this is possible. If we were to begin a simulation with the 1947 parameters and leave them unchanged during a simulation, then the results of the simulation would of course differ from the actual data. This is because we only make use of the 1947 data to compute the 1947 parameters and 1947 might have been an abnormal year. If we were to begin in 1947 and simulate to get a fair test, we would need parameters estimated over a longer period of time than one year. For example, they could be estimated from averaged data for the 1947-74 period. In that case the model (when simulated with these parameters) would be able to generate the average data values for the whole sample period but *not* the actual 1947 data. However, averaging the data is a different parameterization method than we choose to employ.

We believe that since the 1972 parameters were estimated using 1972 information, but no other information, simulating the 1973-78 period does provide a good test of our model, especially because the large changes in the economy since then were not visible in 1972, and in this sense 1972 was an abnormal year. It is not at all obvious that simulating the model beginning in 1947 and using average parameters estimated from the entire sample will provide a tougher test of the model than beginning in 1972 with parameters estimated using only that year's data.

Although most of the parameters which we use in this simulation remain unchanged from 1972, some adjustments must be made. The rates of productivity growth which we employ for each industry are the actual rates that occur in that industry between 1965 and 1972. These rates are assumed to hold over the 1972-78 period. The only other adjustment which we make is to the endowment of labor input. The three skill classes of labor are assumed to grow in the post-72 period at the same rates at which they grew in the 1947-72 period. With these parameter adjustments, we then simulate the model over the years 1972-78.

Tables 3.49 and 3.50 show the percentage differences between the actual data, taken from various July issues of the *Survey of Current Business,* and our projection. The 1972 data will equal the projection for 1972, since 1972 is the start point for this run.

Table 3.49. Percentage Differences in Aggregate Economy Variables (Simulated/Actual)

Year	Gross Private Domestic Investment	PCE	Govt. Purchases	Personal Income Tax Receipts	Private Saving	National Income
1973	-9.2	0.4	-2.0	3.0	-9.5	-1.0
1974	5.4	4.2	-2.0	2.0	-5.8	3.7
1975	40.0	5.7	-1.9	14.9	-7.3	6.6
1976	18.5	2.9	0.05	1.0	-3.4	3.6
1977	7.9	1.3	-0.3	-1.0	-1.3	1.1
1978	3.7	0.5	-0.4	-4.5	-3.7	-2.0

Table 3.50. Percentage Differences in Consumption Goods by Type of Product (Simulated/Actual)

Type of Good	Year					
	1973	1974	1975	1976	1977	1978
Food	3.0	7.8	8.2 *	4.9	3.7	5.9
Clothing	-1.6	2.3	2.5 *	1.0	0.1	-4.1
Personal Care	1.4	8.2	17.6	22.1 *	21.7	20.5
Housing	-2.0 *	-4.7	-6.6	-8.7	-11.9	-14.8
Household Operation	-3.5	-0.7	4.2 *	2.7	0.3	-1.6
Medical Care	-3.2 *	-3.8	-3.3	-6.3	-8.7	-9.7
Personal Business	6.2	10.4	10.7	10.9 *	14.1	9.2
Transport-ation	-1.9	11.8	19.1 *	10.1	6.8	5.4
Recreation + rest.	0.9	3.7	5.8 *	4.2	2.1	-0.5

* Indicates high value.

The percentages listed above are the simulated values as percentages of the actual data. We can see in table 3.49 that for five out of six of the variables listed, the model tends to overpredict and then return to normal. This is understandable, since there was a recession in 1975. This caused the actual 1975 variables to grow less quickly or even to decline. However, our model does not generate a business cycle. Thus the simulated economy continues to grow through the 1975 recession. This causes large divergences between the simulated and the actual situation. This finding also recurs in table 3.50, where five out of nine of the consumption goods show the largest prediction error in 1975.

In the recovery from the 1975 recession, the model's prediction errors decrease substantially. For example, the error in prediction of investment is reduced from 40% to 3.7%, and the prediction error for personal consumption expenditure falls from 5.7% to 0.5%. We can think of this as evidence that the actual economy is returning to the trend rate of growth, which is well predicted by the model.

Turning to table 3.50, we see that consumption goods tend to follow the same pattern as the overall economic variables. However, there is also some evidence of long-run divergence from the actual data for four of the consumption goods. These are personal care, housing, medical care, and personal business. For these four goods, the simulated results seem to diverge continuously or almost continuously from the actual data, even though overall simulated consumption in 1978 is about as close to actual PCE as it was in 1973. These incorrect results are probably due to poor choice of consumption parameters, resulting from bad estimates of elasticities for each of these four goods.

In conclusion, we believe that given the model's limitations, it predicts quite well. The major deficiency in prediction is that our model is unable to generate a business cycle, and thus it would not track the 1975 recession. There are also some problems with estimates for particular consumption goods, which are probably due to poor choices of the relevant elasticities, given that overall simulated consumption is quite close to actual consumption at the end of the period.

Conclusion

The most important simulation performed for this paper was run 2, which assumes zero productivity growth in all industries over the 1947-74 period. This run shows that one of the effects of productivity change on the U.S. economy was to force labor out of agriculture and other industries with high productivity growth and into those sectors (manufacturing, construction, and especially services) where productivity was growing at a slower than average pace. The effect of this on factor shares was to reduce capital's price and share relative to labor. In addition, more highly skilled labor (both white-collar and blue-collar) benefited relative to less highly skilled labor.

The other runs performed tended to reinforce these conclusions. In runs 8 and 9, reducing the dispersion of productivity growth rates reduced the input flows from one sector to another. This is simply an example of the actual flows of inputs in reverse. Other examples of the tendency of inputs to flow out of sectors with high productivity growth are runs 3 through 7, where factor inputs move toward the industry with zero productivity growth and out of the other higher productivity growth industries.

Although actual productivity growth has lowered capital's share and increased that of labor, productivity growth in different sectors has had differing impacts. Runs 3-7 show that given our assumptions, technical change in a particular industry tends to reduce the share of that input in the use of which the industry is intensive. The other effect induced by productivity change is of course the accumulation of capital. Increases in technical change in any particular industry increase capital accumulation which tends to reduce capital's price and share. These two effects combine to give the total effect of productivity change on the distribution of income. Technical change in agriculture hurts unskilled labor relatively to other labor types, while productivity change in manufacturing hurts skilled blue-collar labor (see table 3.33). The only industry in which productivity change reduces the overall labor share is services. This occurs because of the labor intensity of the service sector, and in spite of the induced expansion of the capital stock.

Run 8, where each industry is given an identical rate of growth of productivity, leads to two interesting results. We find that the actual industry pattern of productivity growth has tended to reduce the share of capital more than a more even growth rate would have. In addition, a more even pattern of productivity growth would have benefited unskilled labor relative to skilled labor. This result reinforces our conclusion from run 2 that more skilled labor has benefited from productivity change relative to less skilled labor.

The simulations which we performed have been used to analyze productivity growth and its impacts on the functional distribution of income. In the next chapter, we analyze the impact of productivity change on the accumulation of capital.

4

Induced Accumulation and Productivity Change

Introduction

The analysis of productivity change since Robert Solow's 1957 paper has generally begun by examining the "residual"—that amount of real output growth not explained by the growth of an index of real inputs. Solow's assumptions were that there exists an aggregate production function (and aggregate capital and labor stocks) with constant returns to scale, and that technical progress is Hicks-neutral. In other words, the productivity of both factors is augmented at the same rates. We have:

(4.1) $Q = A[F(K, L)]$.

Under these assumptions, we can equate the residual with the multiplicative parameter associated with Hicks-neutral productivity growth. This measure of technical change does not require the estimation of parameters such as the elasticities of substitution which are hard to pin down. Under the slightly more general assumption of factor augmentation (the factors need not be augmented at the same rates) we have:

(4.2) $Q = F(BK, CL)$

and:

(4.3) $\dot{Q}/Q = M_K[\dot{K}/K] + M_L[\dot{L}/L] + M_K[\dot{B}/B] + M_L[\dot{C}/C]$.

Under these conditions, the residual will still measure technical change, but we will not be able to identify the residual with a single parameter as we can with the Hicks-neutral assumption. With factor augmentation, the residual will still measure technical change, but it will not be independent of the elasticities of substitution or of factor shares.

Once the residual is computed, we know the rate at which the aggregate production function is shifting over time. However, we cannot use the residual to find out the total contribution of productivity change to output growth. Simply computing the number $(\dot{A}/A)/(\dot{Q}/Q)$ can be misleading in two ways. First, this number takes into account the impact of productivity change on capital accumulation. The normal value-added residual is computed as follows:

(4.4) $\dot{A}/A = \dot{Q}/Q - M_K(\dot{K}/K) - M_L[\dot{L}/L].$

This formula treats capital as a primary input like labor. However, we know that since capital is an output of the production process as well as an input, productivity increases that raise output will generally increase capital stock also. The higher capital stock then causes increased output, which feeds back on capital stock and so forth. The conventional residual needs to be adjusted to account for the endogeneity of capital in order to determine the total contribution of productivity change to growth.

The second major reason why the normal value-added residual can be misleading is the effect which productivity change has on intermediate input, which also serves to magnify the effect of technical change. We can compute the total output residual as follows:

(4.5) $\dot{A}'/A' = \dot{O}/O - M_V'[\dot{V}/V] - M_L'[\dot{L}/L] - M_K'[\dot{K}/K]$

where:

(4.6) $O = A'[G(V,L,K)]$ $V =$ intermediate input

$O =$ gross output

Hulten (1978) points out that there is a difference between productivity change originating in a sector, and the impact of productivity change on a sector.[1] The productivity change that originates in a particular sector is simply the rate of change of the sectoral production possibility frontier. However, the impact of productivity change includes the induced shifts of factors between industries and the expansion in intermediate input. We may define these impacts of productivity change as the "effective" rate of productivity change, as opposed to the nominal rates of productivity change. When looking at the importance of productivity change as a source of growth, it is these effects which must be taken into account, since it is the total impact of productivity change on a sector that determines the growth of that sector.

In this paper, we take into account the effect of productivity change, or the response of an economy to shifting technologies and the induced expansion in intermediate input. There have been several previous attempts to account for the endogeneity or reproducibility of capital stock.[2] We go one step further than these attempts by modelling interindustry transactions in our model. In this paper, we will follow the work of Hulten (1975, 1978, 1979). We take endogeneity of capital and intermediate input into account by creating a dynamic model where income is allocated between consumption and investment expenditure over time, and where interindustry transactions occur. By allowing capital and intermediate input to be determined endogeneously, we have a proper framework for determining the overall importance of productivity change for economic growth. When we compare our control solution (run 1) with the zero productivity change run we can see what impact productivity change has had on each sector of the model.

Results

Introduction and First Results

There are several possible methods of computing the contribution of technical change to growth.[3] Suppose that we are unwilling to assume that the U.S. economy actually moves along the long-run growth path (if this path exists). Let us assume instead that the economy is able to achieve a short-run competitive equilibrium at any point in time. In this case, we can define a short-run rate of technical change Z_{SF} (which Hulten terms the short-run Fisherian rate) as the difference between actual growth of real output ($\dot{Q}/Q$) and the rate of growth of real output that would have occurred if technology had remained constant at the level of a given base year ($\dot{Q}^*/Q^*$). Here the "*" indicates what would have occurred in the absence of technical change. We assume that the savings rate is constant, and that technical change is exogeneously determined. Our base year here is 1947. As an approximation, we know that:

$$(4.7) \quad \dot{Q}/Q = \dot{A}/A + M_K(\dot{K}/K) + M_L(\dot{L}/L) \quad (M_K, M_L = K, L \text{ shares in value-added})$$

where the variables are as in the control solution. Also, if technology remains constant, we have:

$$(4.8) \quad \dot{Q}^*/Q^* = M_K^*[\dot{K}^*/K^*] + M_L^*[\dot{L}^*/L^*]$$

where a * indicates variables in the alternate simulation. Our short-run Fisherian rate of technical change is then equal to:

$$(4.9) \quad Z_{SF} = \dot{Q}/Q - \dot{Q}^*/Q^* = \dot{A}/A \quad + [M_K(\dot{K}/K) - M_K^*(\dot{K}^*/K^*)]$$
$$+ [M_L(\dot{L}/L) - M_L^*(\dot{L}^*/L^*)].$$

$\dot{Q}/Q$ measures the actual growth rate of value-added, while $\dot{Q}^*/Q^*$ measures growth due to changing factor inputs, except for the induced accumulation effect. $\dot{Q}/Q$ does include induced capital accumulation. By plugging in actual values for $(\dot{Q}/Q)$ and simulated values for $(\dot{Q}^*/Q^*)$ from run 2 (the zero productivity growth rate run) we can compute Z_{SF}.

Table 4.1 shows the rates of growth of total factor productivity, total output, and the Fisherian residuals and contributions of productivity to growth in the 1947-74 period.

Table 4.1.   Sources of Growth of Real Product, 1947-74 (Average Annual Percentage Growth Rates)

Variable	Conventional	Fisherian
Real Product	3.537%	3.537%
Total Factor Productivity	1.735	2.475
Real Factor Input	1.802	1.063*
Capital	2.930	0.940
Labor	0.936	0.936
Contribution of Technical Change to Growth	.4906	.6996

* We have defined aggregate input as follows:

$$I = [aK^{(s-1)/s} = (1-a)L^{(s-1)/s}]^{s/(s-1)}$$

as in (3.11). Thus we find that:

$$\dot{I}/I = [aK/X]^{(s-1)/s}[\dot{K}/K] + [(1-a)L/X]^{(s-1)/s}[\dot{L}/L]$$
$$+ [s/(s-1)][K^{(s-1)/s} - L^{(s-1)/s}][\dot{a}/X]$$

where:

$$X = aK^{(s-1)/s} = (1-a)L^{(s-1)/s}.$$

Thus we can see that $\dot{I}/I$ is the sum of three terms, two of which represent the changes in K and L, and the third of which represents the change in the distribution parameter a. The growth of Fisherian input is greater than the growth rates of either labor or Fisherian capital because the third term is positive. So in contrast to (3.10) in chapter 3, we here include the $\dot{a}$ term with terms in $\dot{K}/K$ and $\dot{L}/L$.

Since $\dot{K}/K$ will be greater than $\dot{K}^*/K^*$, we will find that Z_{SF} will be greater than the normal residual $(\dot{A}/A)$. Capital inputs will differ between the control and alternate solutions as will capital shares (M_K, M_K^*) and labor shares (M_L, M_L^*), since none of the elasticities of substitution in our model is equal to unity. If, however, the elasticities did equal unity, we would have:

(4.10) $M_K = M_K^*, \qquad M_L = M_L^*.$

Also, we assume that the growth of labor input is unaffected by technical change, which means that:

(4.11) $\dot{L}/L = \dot{L}*/L*.$

Under these conditions, (4.9) reduces to:

(4.12) $Z_{SF} = \dot{A}/A + M_K(\dot{K}/K - \dot{K}*/K*)$

for the total economy. This formulation brings out the main effect which we want to examine, since we would expect that the major difference between the Hicksian residual and the Fisherian rate of productivity change will be the difference in capital accumulation which is induced by the productivity change.

Comparison with Hulten (1975)

We can compare these results with those of Hulten (1975). Using data obtained from L.R. Christensen and D.W. Jorgenson, and using the methods discussed in his 1975 paper, Hulten finds the growth rates of inputs, outputs, and productivity to be as listed in table 4.2. These growth rates differ from my own due to two main causes: differences in time period, and differences in the methods used to derive the underlying output and input quantities. The growth rates listed in table 4.3 represent growth rates of the same variables over the same time period as the previous table, but using my data. Although my real product growth rate is not far from that computed from the Christensen-Jorgenson data over the period 1948-66, my real factor input growth rates are below, and my technical change growth rate is above that of Christensen and Jorgenson. Since there are differences in input aggregation and in other methods between Christensen-Jorgenson and myself, this difference is not surprising.

The difference between the contribution of technical change to growth as conventionally measured (49%) and the Fisherian contribution of technical change to growth (70%) is approximately 21% in my simulation. This contrasts with the 30% difference between the conventional contribution of technical change to growth and the Fisherian contribution as determined by Hulten (1975). This difference is caused by several things. First, we use a six sector model and elasticities of substitution that are not equal to unity, while Hulten uses only two sectors (consumption and investment) and assumes unitary elasticities of substitution.[4] In addition, the data sources which we use are different. Thus our results, while differing in some details from Hulten's work, sustain his conclusion that "the induced accumulation effect is a potentially important source of economic growth..." and that when "these induced effects are allowed for, technical change is seen to be potentially far more important than heretofore thought."[5]

Table 4.2.   Sources of Growth of Real Product, 1948-66 (Average
Annual Percentage Growth Rates Computed Using
Christensen-Jorgenson Data)

Variable	Christensen–Jorgenson	Fisherian
Real Product	4.15	4.15
Real Factor Input	2.73	1.48
Capital	4.22	1.49
Labor	1.50	1.50
Technical change	1.42	2.67
Contribution of Technical Change to Growth	0.34	0.64

Table 4.3.   Sources of Growth of Real Product, 1948-66 (Average
Annual Percentage Growth Rates Computed Using Our Data)

Variable	Conventional	Fisherian
Real Product	3.8567	3.8567
Real Factor Input	1.3498	0.6099
Capital	2.7127	0.8529
	+	+
Labor	0.511	0.4543
Technical Change	2.5069	3.2468
Contribution of Technical Change to Growth	0.65	0.84

+   The differences in growth of labor between the two simulations is due to differences in the prices of labor, and to reallocations of labor between industries.

Further Results: Long-Run Fisherian Rate of Technical Change

In deriving our short run rate of technical change (Z_{SF}) we assumed that the economy achieves a short-run competitive equilibrium at any point in time. If we wish to make stronger assumptions, we may examine a model of optimal growth where the economy is always on its long-run growth path at each point in time.[6] We define the endowment available at the beginning of each period

K_{t+1} as a linear homogeneous function of the previous period's endowment not consumed $(K_t - C_t)$ and labor input L_t:

(4.13) $K_{t+1} = F[K_t - C_t, L_t]$.

If consumers in such an economy maximize the discounted sum of consumption over time, then the optimal consumption plan for such an economy is the solution to the problem:

(4.14) Maximize $U = \sum_{t=0}^{\infty} a^t u[C_t / L_t]$

with respect to $C_0, C_1, C_2, \ldots$, subject to:

(4.15) $K_{t+1} / L_{t+1} = F_i[K_t - C_t, L_t]$;

   $i = 0, 1, 2, \ldots$ = states of technology;

(4.16) $L_{t+1} = n[L_t]$ $(t = 0, 1, 2, \ldots$ = time periods)

where C_t is consumption per time period, L_t is labor input, K_t is capital, n is a labor growth rate, and "a" is a subjective discount factor. Assuming that the economy can achieve a unique stationary optimum $(\bar{K}_i, \bar{C}_i)$ for each level of technology F_i, the stationary values satisfy:

(4.17) $1.0/a = \dot{F}_i[\bar{K}_i - \bar{C}_i, \bar{L}_i]$;

(4.18) $\bar{K}_i = F_i[\bar{K}_i - \bar{C}_i, \bar{L}_i]$.

If the technology shifts sufficiently smoothly, we can define the path of long run per capita optimal output $[\bar{K}_i(t) / \bar{L}_i(t)] = \bar{k}(t)$ from the above two equations. Hulten points out that a movement along the $k(t)$ path takes into account the induced accumulation effect, and defines the long run rate of technical change.[8] We can differentiate (4.17) totally:

(4.19) $\dot{\bar{k}}/\bar{k} = M_K[(\dot{\bar{k}} - \dot{\bar{C}})/(\bar{k} - \bar{C})] + [\dot{A}/A]$.

We then use a result of Diamond (1965) that:

(4.20) $[(\dot{\bar{k}} - \dot{\bar{C}})/(\bar{k} - \bar{C})] = [s/(1 - M_K)][\dot{A}/A]$

   $+ s$ [Hicksian bias of technical change]

where $\dot{A}/A$ is the normal growth of Hicks-neutral productivity. We can then derive the long run rate of technical change (Z_{LF}) which Hulten terms the "long run Fisherian" rate.[8] This is given by:

(4.21) $Z_{LF} = [1.0 + sM_K/(1.0 - M_K)] \, (\dot{A}/A)$

for the Hicks-neutral case where the bias of technical change is zero. Although to apply this formula to our model we have assumed Hicks neutrality, nothing in this derivation assumes this. If we want to take non Hicks neutral progress into account, we simply add the term sM_K(bias) onto the right hand side of (4.21).

We can see that Z_{LF} is greater than the conventional residual, since the term in parentheses in (4.21) is greater than unity. To compute Z_{LF}, we simply substitute the actual economy-wide values for the aggregate capital share, the economy-wide elasticity of substitution, and an aggregate rate of technical change into (4.21). Table 4.4 shows that the total contribution of technical change to growth when computed in this way is 66.2%. This result may, of course, suffer from aggregation bias.

Table 4.4.   Average Annual Growth Rates, 1947-74

	$\dot{A}/A$	Z_{LF}	$\dot{Q}/Q$
Total Economy	1.735	2.342	3.537
Contribution of Technical Change to Growth	0.4906	0.6621	

Effective Rates of Productivity Change: Total Economy

So far we have derived measures of the effect of productivity change on growth for the overall economy. We can also compute the total impact of technical change on the economy on a sectoral basis. In other words, we can compute the sectoral "effective" rates of productivity change. We measure these sectorally as the difference between the actual growth of output and the rate of growth of output occurring when no productivity change takes place. In mathematical terms, where Z_E is the effective rate of productivity change:

(4.22) $Z_{SF} = \dot{Q}/Q - \dot{Q}^*/Q^* = \dot{Q}/Q - \dot{I}^*/I^*$;   * = alternate solution

and:

(4.23) $Q^* = H(L^*, K^*) = I^*$;   and $\dot{Q}^*/Q^* = \dot{I}^*/I^*$.

Table 4.5 shows the sectoral and aggregate effective rates of productivity change, and compares then to the actual rates.[9]

Table 4.5. Average Annual Growth Rates of Productivity: Sectoral Effective and Actual Rates, 1947-74

Industry	Actual Rate[+] $(\dot{A}/A)$	Effective Rate $(\dot{Z}_E)$	Output Growth $(\dot{Q}/Q)$
Agric.	2.8093	1.7209	1.149
Miscel.	1.4487	2.0079	3.808
Constr.	1.8264	4.3221	3.053
Manuf.	2.1125	3.1247	3.455
Equip.	2.1752	2.3673	3.666
Serv.	1.5784	2.7724	3.322
Total	1.735	2.4745	3.537
Contribution of Technical Change to Growth	0.4906	0.6996	

[+] Productivity change computed using value-added base.

Hulten (1978) points out that one can find the total effect of productivity change on output (Z_E) in two different ways. One can aggregate the effective rates of productivity change $[Z_{Ei}/Z_{Ei}]$, using a weighted average of their sectoral shares in value-added. This gives the following equation:[10]

$$(4.24) \quad Z_E = \sum_{i=1}^{6} \left| p_i Q_i \middle/ \sum_{i=1}^{6} p_i Q_i \right| (\dot{Z}_{Ei}/Z_{Ei})$$

where:

$$(4.25) \quad O_i = Q_i + \sum_{j=1}^{6} V_{ij}$$

O = total output

Q = value added

V = intermediate input

In addition, we have:

$$(4.26) \quad Z_E = \sum_{i=1}^{6} \left| p_i O_i \right| \Big/ \sum_{i=1}^{6} \left| p_i Q_i \right| \ (\dot{A}/A)$$

which is a weighted *sum* of the conventional residuals, with the weights summing to more than unity. The reason that the weights sum to more than one is that "the change in sectoral factor efficiency creates, in general, extra output..., which serves to increase both final demand...and intermediate deliveries...The increase in intermediate deliveries, however, serves further to increase output in those sectors using the intermediate good, and this further increases output in those sectors using the intermediate good, and this further increases output, and so on."[11] Hulten (1978) shows that these two methods for computing the total effect of technical change on the economy are equivalent.

When we compare table 4.5 with table 4.4, the aggregate economy rates of effective productivity change should agree, and they do approximately (2.4745 to 2.342). Thus a third means of accounting for the induced capital accumulation effect has resulted in an estimate (69.96 percent) of the contribution of productivity change to growth which is in agreement with the other two methods (66.21 percent for the long-run Fisherian rate and 69.96 percent for the short-run Fisherian rate).

Our simulations have thus confirmed the overall importance of technical change as a source of growth. Technical change has been shown to have a much greater impact on the growth of output than had been thought before Hulten's work appeared (1975, 1978, 1979), and Hulten's conclusions have been confirmed by our results. However, so far in this chapter we have simply compared our results with those of Hulten in his 1975 paper. We have not yet taken into account the later results (Hulten 1978, 1979) in this area. We now proceed to do so.

Intertemporal Accounting and the Importance of Productivity Change

We can define the conventional residual as the "growth rate of real product not explained by the share-weighted growth rates of the real factor inputs."[12] We can also point out that the "analysis of productivity change typically starts with a detailed description of the accounting framework used in the calculations. The appropriate accounting identities are first developed, and then differentiated to obtain the productivity residual."[13] A simple example of this is the following:

$$(4.27) \quad PQ = WI \qquad \text{and} \qquad A = Q/I = W/P$$

and:

(4.28) $\dot{A}/A = \dot{Q}/Q - \dot{I}/I = \dot{W}/W - \dot{P}/P$

where P and W are aggregate output and input prices, and Q and I are aggregate output and input quantities, respectively. This is the conventional residual, and the input measure I above includes capital. However, we recognize that the input measure above treats capital input as a primary input, while in fact capital input is an intermediate input and must be measured in a dynamic (capital endogenous) framework. Hulten has derived such a framework, and we move now to discuss it.[14]

Let us begin by defining the value of product originating in each period in a one-good economy without a government or foreign sector:

(4.29) $p_t Q_t = p_t C_t + p_t I_t$

I = investment

C = consumption

Q = value added

In addition, we also have:

(4.30) $p_t Q_t = w_t L_t + r_t K_{t-1}$

L = labor input

K = capital input

r = rental price of K

We can define the capital stock in any period as follows:

(4.31) $K_t = I_t + (1 - d)K_{t-1} = I_t + (1 - d)I_{t-1} + (1 - k)K_{t-2} = \ldots$

or, in other words, capital stock is defined using a perpetual inventory definition with a constant depreciation rate. The rental prices of capital can be related to the final sales price of a unit of capital (p_t) as follows:

(4.32) $p_{t-1} = r_t + (1 - d)p_t = r_t + (1 - d)r_{t+1} + (1 - d)^2 p_{t+1} = \ldots$

In other words, p_t is the discounted flow of rental prices (net of depreciation) plus the end of period value of the good.

We can also rewrite (4.29) in order to split the total value of product into deliveries to intermediate demand and deliveries to final demand. We define intermediate demand in this intertemporal model as the value of investment delivered from period t to production in each subsequent period, while final demand is the value of consumption plus that amount of investment that is carried over, or exported to the future at the end of the period. For example, if $t = 1$, and we are considering a four period model as an example, with remaining capital stock after that period considered as final demand, we have:

$$(4.33) \quad p_1 Q_1 = [p_1 C_1 + p_4(1 - d)^3 I_1] + [r_2 I_1 + r_3(1 - d)I_1$$
$$+ r_4(1 - d)^2 I_1]$$

where the first bracketed term on the right hand side of the equation is final demand in this accounting framework, and the second term is a delivery to intermediate demand. We treat endogeneously produced capital as an intermediate good. This equation represents the uses side of national product.

The value of product can also be considered on the sources side. We can break down (4.30) into the value of intermediate input and the value of primary input. Labor input ($w_t L_t$) is considered as primary input, as is the importation of capital from the past at time $t[r_t(1-d)^{t-1} K_0]$. The sum of deliveries of investment goods from past periods to period t is treated here as intermediate input. For example, if $t = 4$, in a four period model, we have:

$$(4.34) \quad p_4 Q_4 = [w_4 L_4 + r_4(1 - d)^3 K_0] + [r_4 I_3 + r_4(1 - d)I_2 + r_4(1 - d)^2 I_1].$$

The first bracketed term is primary input, and the second is intermediate input here. We know that the sum of final demand is equal to the sum of primary input, or:

$$(4.35) \quad \sum p_t C_t + \sum p_4(1 - d)^{4-t} I_t = \sum w_t L_t + \sum r_t(1 - d)^{t-1} K_0.$$

Using (4.31) and (4.32) for K_t and p_t, we find that (for a four-period model):

$$(4.36) \quad \sum_{t=1}^{4} p_t C_t + p_4 K_4 - p_0 K_0 = \sum_{t=1}^{4} w_t L_t = \overline{W}_4.$$

Here we may define $\overline{W}_4$, which is the net addition to wealth accumulated during the simulation period ($t = 0, \ldots, 4$), as being equal to the sum of consumption and the net increase of capital over our period, or in other words, the left hand side of (4.36). This is our basic intertemporal accounting identity which treats capital as an intermediate input, and it is analogous to the conventional result that GNP measured on the expenditure and the income side is identical. Total value-added is equal to total labor input since capital goods are treated as intermediate.

We can extend this result from four to N periods to give:

(4.37) $\quad \overline{W}_N = \sum_{t=0}^{N} p_t C_t + p_N K_N - p_0 K_0 = \sum_{t=0}^{N} w_t L_t.$

We can then differentiate (5.36) with respect to time to derive a dynamic productivity residual. This is computed as follows:

(4.38) $\quad T(O,N) = \sum_{t=0}^{N} (p_t C_t / \overline{W}_N) [\dot{C}_t / C_t] + (p_N K_N / \overline{W}_N) [\dot{K}_N / K_N]$

$$- (p_0 K_0 / \overline{W}_N) [\dot{K}_0 / K_0] - \sum_{t=0}^{N} (w_t L_t / W_N)[\dot{L}_t / L_t].$$

This is the residual growth in wealth not accounted for by the growth of primary input for the period as a whole, where the capital stock is not considered as a primary input.[15] It takes into account the endogeneity of the capital stock, and we expect it to be larger than the normal residual.

Hulten also shows that the dynamic residual is a linear combination of the conventional residuals as follows:

(4.39) $\quad T(O,N) = \sum_{t=0}^{N} [p_t Q_t / \overline{W}_N] (T_i^*)$

where T_i^* is defined as:

(4.40) $\quad T_i^* = \dot{Q}_t / Q_t - \left[\dfrac{w_t L_t}{p_t Q_t} \right] [\dot{L}_t / L_t] - \left[\dfrac{r_t K_{t-1}}{p_t Q_t} \right] [\dot{K}_{t-1} / K_{t-1}].$

Input weights in (4.40) are labor and capital shares.

Table 4.6 gives us the values of the dynamic residuals computed according to (4.38) and (4.39). We can see from this table that the contribution of technical change to growth when computed in this way is between 70.7% and 71.9%. However, the ratio of aggregate productivity growth computed using (4.39) to the growth of value-added is only 52.6%. Thus the induced accumulation effect accounts for between 19.3% and 21.6% of the total growth of output.[16] Using gross output rather than value-added changes these results only slightly, as we can see from rows 7 and 8 in table 4.6. This is because the rate of growth of gross output is only slightly below that of value-added.

Table 4.6. Average Annual Growth Rates of Productivity, Output, and
Contribution of Productivity Growth to Output Growth[+]

Row	Value	Equation 4.38	Equation 4.39
1)	$T(0,N)$	2.501	2.542
2)	$\dot{Q}_t/Q_t$	3.537	3.537
3)	Contribution of technical change to value-added growth =(1)/(2)	70.69%	71.87%
4)	$T_t{}^*$		1.859
5)	$T_t{}^*/[\dot{Q}_t/Q_t]$		52.56%
6)	$\dot{O}_t/O_t$	3.509	3.509
7)	Contribution of technical change to gross output growth =(1)/(6)	71.26%	72.44%
8)	$T_t{}^*/[\dot{O}_t/O_t]$		52.98%

+   Values are in terms of percentage growth rates per year, unless otherwise indicated.

This section has shown that when we compute the importance of productivity change to growth in a totally different manner the results are approximately the same as in the previous section. This is what we had expected, and this result substantiates our confidence in the validity of our work.

Sectoral Effective Rates of Productivity Change

We have previously mentioned the concept of an effective rate of productivity change. Earlier we measured this as the difference between the actual rate of growth of output and that rate of growth of output which occurs when no productivity change takes place. In this section, we make use of the result that the overall effective rate of productivity growth [as given in (4.24)] can be computed from the sectoral productivity residuals. In other words, we have:

$$(4.24) \quad Z_E = \sum_{i=1}^{6} \left[p_i O_i \Big/ \sum_{i=1}^{6} p_i Q_i \right] [\dot{A}_i / A_i]$$

The weights in (4.24) sum to more than one.

As in the previous section, we will treat capital as an intermediate input, so that the only primary input is labor. Our residuals here will be total output residuals. We have:

$$(4.41) \quad \dot{A}_i' / A_i' = \dot{O}_i / O_i - M_L' [\dot{L}_i / L_i] - M_K' [\dot{K}_i / K_i] - M_V' [\dot{V}_i / V_i].$$

The residuals used in table 4.5 were on a value-added base which are equivalent to (4.41) with the deletion of the $\dot{V}_i / V_i$ term.

We then substitute total output residuals, gross output, and labor input into (4.24). Table 4.7 shows the results. Computed in this way, the overall effective rate of technical change is 2.56% per year. Productivity growth is responsible for 72.42% of growth, according to this computation. This compares with the other estimates of from 69.96% to 71.87%. The new and slightly different computation of the importance of productivity change for growth is in the same range as the previous estimates, and it also helps to reinforce our conclusions about the importance of the induced accumulation effect.

Table 4.7. Computation of Overall Effective Rates of
Productivity Change

Industry	Gross Output Residuals (% per year)	Weights as in (7)	Product of Col. 1 and 2	Value-added weights
Agric.	1.1193	.13265	.1484	.0311
Misc.	0.9947	1.03734	1.0319	.4797
Constr.	0.5879	.13533	.0796	.0306
Manuf.	0.8002	.89938	.7197	.2400
Equip.	0.9137	.25428	.2323	.0754
Serv.	0.9060	.38597	.3497	.1431
Total	0.9207	2.84496	2.5617	1.000

Conclusion

In this chapter we have examined the importance of productivity change in the growth process. Using several different concepts and methods of measurement, we have found that productivity change accounts for between 66.21% and 72.42% of economic growth. We think the low estimate using (4.21) is probably biased downward due to aggregation bias. On the other hand, using conventional methods of determining the importance of productivity change to growth results in estimates of between 49.06% and 52.6%. Thus the importance of the induced accumulation effect is verified, and its magnitude using our methods and data is put at about 20%.

Appendix

Notation

The symbol on the left (A for example) is the symbol whose usage is described in the phrase to the right, along with the pages where the symbol is employed, if it is not used throughout the study. Some symbols are used more than once. Generally this usage occurs in different chapters. There will be four different types of symbols used: capitalized letters, uncapitalized letters, capitalized Greek letters, and uncapitalized Greek letters. The Greek letters are reserved for those terms which are less often employed.

Capitalized Letters

A. Hicksian productivity parameter.

B. Capital augmentation parameter.

C. Consumption demands.
    Labor augmentation parameter.

D. Divisia index.

E. Market demands.

F. Distribution function of returns, and production functions.

G. Production function.

H. Production function.
    Intermediate input matrix (chapter 1 only).

I. Identity matrix.
    Index sets (chapter 2 footnotes only).
    Overall input.

J. Index sets (chapter 2 footnotes only).

K. Capital in a sector or industry.

L. Stock of labor in a sector or industry.

M. Factor shares in value added where subscript indicates factor, e.g. $M_K = 1.0 - M_L$ is capital share in value-added. We use a "'" to indicate factor shares in gross output. Thus M_V' is intermediate input share in gross output and $M_V = 1.0 - M_L' - M_L'$.

O. Gross output.

P. Vector of output prices.

Q. Value-added.

R. Total tax revenue.

S. Overall savings.

T. Dynamic residual. T_i^* will also be used to represent the conventional residual.

U. Utility.

V. Intermediate output.

W. Overall input prices (chapter 1 and 3). We will also use the term $\overline{W}$ to represent the addition to wealth over the sample period in chapter 4.

X. Term defined in chapter 1.
    Vector of inputs.

Y. Consumer disposable income.

Z. Effective rates of productivity change.
    Also, a term defined in chapter 3.

Uncapitalized Letters

a. Constant elasticity of substitution production function parameter.

c. Cobb-Douglas function exponents for capital aggregation from structures and equipment stocks.

d. Depreciation rates.

e. The average rate of productivity change.

g. Cobb-Douglas function exponents for labor aggregation from different skill classes of labor.

h. Individual elements of the H matrix of intermediate inputs.

i. Index of individual industries, goods, etc.

j. Index of individual industries, goods, etc.

k. Capital-labor ratio.

l. Index of individual persons.

m. Required demands in the linear expenditure demand system.

n. Growth rate of labor input (chapter 4 only).

p. Output prices.

q. Purchase price of capital good.

r. Capital rental prices.
    Also, row factors in RAS model (chapter 2 only).

s. Elasticity of substitution.
    Also, column factors in RAS model (chapter 2 only).

t. Tax rates, with subscripts indicating precisely which good or factor is being taxed. For example, t_K is a factor tax on capital.

u. Row sums of the matrix to which the RAS model is being applied (chapter 2 only).
    Also, utility functions for individual time periods in a long run growth model (chapter 4 only).

v. Column sums of the matrix to which the RAS model is being applied (chapter 2 only).

w. Labor input price (wage).

x. Input quantities.

y. The product of the investment tax credit, the corporate income tax rate, and the present value of depreciation deductions (chapter 2 only).

z. The present value of depreciation deductions on capital (chapter 2 only).

Greek Letter Notation (Uncapitalized)

α (alpha)   Demand parameter in the linear expenditure demand system.

β (beta)   Demand parameter in the linear expenditure demand system.

κ (kappa)   An individual's portfolio (chapter 1 only).

η (eta)   Input-output coefficent.

μ (mu)   Expected value of returns on a portfolio.

ν (nu)   Rate of return on capital goods.

ξ (xi)   Elasticities.

σ (sigma)   The variance of returns (when squared) of an individual's portfolio (chapter 1 only).

τ (tau)   The percentage of an individual's portfolio invested in any particular asset (chapter 1 only).

ω (omega)   Elements of the G-matrix relating consumption classified by industry (agriculture, manufacturing) to consumption classified by type of good (food, clothing, etc.).

Greek Letter Notation (Capitalized)

Ω (omega)   G-matrix relating consumption by the producer good classification to consumption by the consumption good type (food, clothing, etc.).

Notes

Chapter 1

1.   See Solow (1958), Denison (1962, 1967, 1972, 1974), Jorgenson and Griliches (1967, 1972), Kendrick (1961, 1973), Star (1974), Christensen and Jorgenson (1969, 1970), Chinloy (1978), and Gollop and Jorgenson (1977) for recent U.S. productivity work.

2.   We might also assume a more general factor augmenting function as follows:

$$Q = F[BK, CL]$$

and:

$$\dot{Q}/Q - M_K[\dot{K}/K] - M_L(\dot{L}/L) = \text{Residual} = M_K(\dot{B}/B) + M_L(\dot{C}/C).$$

If $\dot{B}/B$ is equal to $\dot{C}/C$, we have Hicks-neutrality. In this more general case, the residual will still be a valid measure of technical change, but we will not be able to equate productivity change with the growth of a single parameter, as we can with the Hicks-neutrality assumption. Under these factor augmenting assumptions, the residual will not be independent of the elasticities of substitution, nor of factor shares, but it will measure technical change.

    We should also note that throughout this work we maintain the assumption of linear homogeneity, or constant returns to scale. In other words, given equation (1.2), we may derive:

(1.2′) $tQ = AtF(K,L) = AF(tK,tL)$

where t is any factor. We thus rule out increasing returns to scale as a source of growth. We believe that empirical evidence of increasing returns to scale may actually measure changes in input quality [see Griliches (1964)], or short-run business cycle fluctuations [see Fair (1969) or Griliches (1979)]. Thus we do not deal with increasing returns.

3.   Solow (1957), pp. 312-20.

4.   We are assuming that labor inputs are not endogenous to the economic system.

5.   Hulten has analyzed this problem in three papers (1975, 1978, 1979).

6.   The following analysis closely follows Hulten (1975).

7. To see this for a simple example, let equation (1.2) become

    (1.2') $Q_t = A_t[K_t]^{a1}[L_t]^{a2}$; $a_1 + a_2 = 1.$

    If we divide Q_{t1} (the line Ob) by Q_{t0} (the line Oac), we have:

    $$A_{t1}/A_{t0} = [Q_{t1}/Q_{t0}] / [(K_{t1}/K_{t0})^{a1}(L_{t1}/L_{t0})^{a0}].$$

    Taking logarithms and differentiating:

    $$\dot{A}/A = \dot{Q}/Q - a_1[\dot{K}/K] - a_2[\dot{L}/L] = \dot{Q}/Q - M_K[\dot{K}/K] - M_L[\dot{L}/L]$$

    because of our assumption that factors are being paid their marginal products. Thus the residual in this case (which has constant factor shares) in an exact measure of the rise in factor efficiency, which can be represented in our diagram by the shift upward in the production function. In the more general case, the residual is an excellent approximation to the underlying rate of growth of productivity. It is an approximation, since we are calculating a discrete approximation to a continuous index, and the two will not be exactly equal unless shares are unchanged.

8. See Hicks (1965), T.K. Rymes (1968, 1971), L.M. Read (1968), and Hulten (1975, 1979).

9. Hulten (1975).

10. For an alternative analysis of the same data, using some different assumptions, see Christensen and Jorgenson (1969, 1970, 1973).

11. We assume here that technical change is exogeneously determined. We do not think that any inaccuracies are introduced by this assumption, given the serious problems in finding out what determines technical change.

12. See George F. Break, "The Incidence and Economic Effects of Taxation," pp. 119-237 in *The Economics of Public Finance,* The Brookings Institution, 1974, Washington, D.C., especially p. 127.

13. Scarf (1973), p. 10.

14. For discussion of Scarf's algorithm, see Scarf (1967, 1969, 1973). For recent uses of the algorithm, see Shoven (1976), Shoven and Whalley (1972, 1973, 1977), Whalley (1975a, 1975b, 1977), and King (1977, 1980) among others. For proofs of existence of equilibrium, see Shoven and Whalley (1973), and Shoven (1974).

15. Scarf (1973), p. 16.

16. This model is discussed in Deaton and Brown (1972), pp. 1195-1200. We are dealing here with *ordinal* utility, not *cardinal* utility, and thus a monotonic transformation of the utility function leaves us with the same utility function. We are determining only the extra, or supernumary consumption over and above the m_i. In the maximization problem, we take the derivative with respect to $(C_i - m_i)$, not simply C_i.

17. Direct additivity implies a proportionality between the own price and income elasticities, while indirect additivity implies that the sum of income and price elasticities is a constant.

18. Deaton (1974), p. 345.

19. In this context, we can also refer to the Modigliani-Miller analysis: Modigliani, Franco, and Miller, Merton H. "The Cost of Capital, Corporation Finance, and the Theory of

Investment." *American Economic Review*, June 1958, **48**, no. 3, 261-97. They show that the market value of any firm is independent of its capital structure (i.e. debt-equity ratio), and discuss the consequences of the corporate income tax for equity, debt, and internal financing of investments. However, in our model, we do not have alternative financial arrangements, and so this analysis is not relevant.

20. As opposed to David and Scadding (1974) and Denison (1958), Feldstein (1974) suggests that the empirically observed constancy of the gross private saving rate has no behavioral significance. He believes that the rising incomes in the U.S. have tended to increase saving, but that saving has decreased due to the effects of the social security system. He also thinks that these effects have then tended to exactly cancel each other, although why they should exactly cancel is unclear. Of course, there are probably other forces operating which would tend to change the saving rate. However, as a simplifying assumption, we accept the constancy of the saving rate, along with the validity of the bulk of the empirical evidence.

21. The factor demands listed above are those for the assumption of Hicks-neutrality. We increase A in (1.11), (1.16), and (1.18) to denote the effects of Hicks-neutral productivity change. However, it is also possible to model the effects of Harrod neutrality. We can then apply the same simulation techniques to compute the effects of Harrod-neutral technical change.

22. Berndt and Christensen (1974), pp. 339-40.

23. See Jorgenson (1966) for a more detailed discussion of this point.

24. Burmeister and Dobell (1970), chapter 3.

25. Uzawa (1961), p. 123.

26. Let $\bar{C}_t$ represent consumption in the following equations. If H is linearly homogeneous in $\bar{C}_{t+1}, \ldots \bar{C}_{t+n}$, then there exists an ideal price deflator $\bar{P}(p_1, \ldots, p_n)$ for money outlay $\Sigma_{t+1}^{t+n} p_t C_t$, so that we can form a reduced utility function $V(C_0, D)$, where:

(a) $D = H(C_{t+1}, \ldots, C_{t+n}) = [\sum_{t+1}^{t+n} p_t C_t / P]$.

Then working only with V and a budget line:

(b) $W = \bar{C}_0 + \bar{P}D$,

the correct optimal values of consumption and capital accumulation can be determined.

27. See Shoven and Whalley (1977) for a justification of this, on pp. 217-18.

28. If an investor maximizes a utility function which depends on mean (μ) and variance (σ^2) of a portfolio, i.e. $U = U(\mu, \sigma^2)$, $U_\mu > 0$, $U_{\sigma^2} < 0$, then he will never take an actuarially fair bet. If, however, $U = U(\mu, \sigma^2, M_3)$, where M_3 is the third moment of the distribution, and the derivative of U with respect to M_3 is not zero, then some actuarially fair bets will be accepted.

29. See Tsiang (1972), p. 362.

30. Tsiang lists the assumptions which an appropriate utility function $U(W)$ for a risk-averse individual ought to have:

(i) $U_{\bar{W}}$ positive—positive marginal utility of wealth.

(ii) $U_{\bar{W}\bar{W}}$ negative—decreasing marginal utility of wealth.

(iii) $[\dot{U}_{\overline{W}\overline{W}}/U_{\overline{W}}] \leqq 0$ —marginal absolute risk aversion should decrease with wealth (a dot over the variable indicates differentiation with respect to wealth).

(iv) $[-\overline{W}\dot{U}_{\overline{W}\overline{W}}/U_{\overline{W}}] \geqq 0$ —marginal relative risk aversion should increase with increases in wealth.

31.   For example, if we are given:

$$U(\mu, \sigma^2) = a_0\mu - a_1 \sigma^2;$$

$$\sigma_{EE} = \Sigma_{SS} = 1, \sigma_{ES} = 1/2, a_0 = 10, a_1 = 1, \nu_E = .1, \nu_S = .08$$

then $\tau_E = 5(\nu_E - \nu_S) + 1/2 = .0.6.$

Chapter 2

1.   For example, if wage payments to labor were $10000, but labor income was $12000, when simulating the model the final solution would probably not be either of these two numbers, but some other number. This discrepancy might affect other numbers which we knew were correct. If this happened, it would imply that the original numbers fed into the algorithm were not an equilibrium. If they had been the algorithm would have converged to the original data. If the original situation were not an equilibrium then we could not be sure that our comparisons of different simulation runs with the original situation had meaning.

2.   See John Whalley and John Piggott (1977) for a list of consistency assumptions and a discussion.

3.   A reconciliation is available in the *Survey of Current Business* (1973).

4.   See the *National Income and Product Accounts of the U.S., 1929-1974, Statistical Tables,* Bureau of Economic Analysis, 1977.

5.   See Christensen and Jorgenson (1970).

6.   See Christensen (1971).

7.   Kravis (1959).

8.   Other labor income consists mainly of employers' contributions to private pension funds, along with other miscellaneous items.

9.   Christensen and Jorgenson (1973).

10.   Mieskowski (1972).

11.   Shoven and Whalley (1972).

12.   Some of these taxes are motor vehicle taxes, sales taxes, excise taxes, and nontaxes (i.e., state university tuition).

13.   Jack Faucett Associates (1975), prepared for the Bureau of Labor Statistics.

14.   See Whalley (1977a).

15.   *NIPA Statistical Tables,* p. viii.

16.   See *National Income and Product Accounts, Statistical Tables* (1977), p. ix.

17.   *National Income and Product Accounts Statistical Tables,* pp. vi-viii (definition of other labor income).

18. See Whalley and Piggott, p. 18.

19. R.R. Nelson and S.G. Winter, "Dynamic Competition and Technical Progress." In *Economic Progress, Private Values, and Public Policy*, edited by B. Balassa and R.R. Nelson, North-Holland, New York, 1977.

20. See Shoven and Whalley (1972) and Whalley and Piggott (1977) on this point. We employ a factor of 1000 and divide the endowments by that number, enabling us to use data denominated in millions, rather than in thousands.

21. We are assuming that industry requirements for raw materials, semi-finished products and finished products are proportional to output.

22. The first Christensen-Jorgenson study (1969) derived a land price change figure of 6.9%. What this figure is derived from is not discussed.

23. Christensen and Jorgenson (1969), pp. 293-311.

24. Ibid. (1969), pp. 304-5.

25. Ibid.

26. *National Income and Product Accounts, Statistical Tables* (1977), pp. 294-96, 353.

27. Christensen-Jorgenson (1969), *NIPA Statistical Tables* (1977), and Goldsmith (1951).

28. Ibid.

29. Shoven and Whalley (1974), p. 476.

30. Ibid.

31. Census (1970), and Bureau of Labor Statistics (1977). The BLS data break up occupation ten.

32. Scarf (1973).

33. Gollop and Jorgenson (1977). This data was developed using the RAS model, and thus the accuracy of each individual cell may be questionable.

34. M.A. King (1972).

35. The 1972 Input-Output tables have since become available. See the *Survey of Current Business*, February 1979 and April 1979 issues.

36. See *Survey of Current Business* (1970), (1965), (1969), and (1974). Agriculture corresponds to I-O classifications 1-4, manufacturing to I-O industries 13-64, services to I-O industries 72-77, "other" to 5-10 and 65-71, structures-producing to 11-12, and equipment-producing to those parts of the other industries which were devoted to producing equipment for gross private capital formation.

37. See E.F. Denison *Accounting for U.S. Economic Growth, 1929-1969*, pp. 62-65.

38. Shoven and Whalley (1974), p. 345.

39. For a discussion of this model, see Bacharach (1965).

40. Ibid.

41. Especially, if we have index sets I', I, J', J, where: $I' \cup I = 1, 2, \ldots, n$; I' intersect $I =$ null set, $J' \cup J = 1, 2, \ldots, m$; J' intersect $J =$ null set; then these index sets form a partition of the row and column indices. If $A_{I'J} = 0$ implies that:

$$\sum_{i \in I'} u_i = \sum_{j \in J} v_j \quad \text{and} \quad \sum_{i \in I} u_i = \sum_{j \in J'} v_j$$

then the process will converge.

42. Gollop and Jorgenson apply this convergence criterion. See Gollop and Jorgenson (1977).

43. There were other adjustments made to the data in order to make the input-output tables conform to each other. We converted the I-O tables to a domestic output base by deducting the domestic port value of transferred imports from the industry row totals, and then treating imports as a negative final demand column. Normally, the I-O tables are on a total output base, where imports appear as a row of the I-O table, and are thus included in row and column totals. In addition, to maintain comparability between the input-output tables and our gross product originating (value-added) data, we added industry 86 (household industry, i.e., domestic service) to the services sector. We also added industries 81-83 (business travel, entertainment and gifts, office supplies, and scrap and used goods) to services.

44. See BEA (1975), and *Survey of Current Business* (1970), (1965), (1969), and (1974).

Chapter 3

1. In addition to Hicks-neutrality, one often used assumption on the form of technical change is Harrod-neutrality. This can be represented by the rise in the parameter A_H in the following equation:

$$Q = [a_H K^{s-1/s} + (1 - a_H)(A_H L)^{(s-1)/s}]^{s/(s-1)}.$$

The subscript H denotes parameters chosen for a Harrod-neutral specification of technical progress. This specification of the production function implies that if A_H only grows, factor shares are constant for a given capital-output ratio. This means that if we can measure the optimum length of production processes by K/Q, for any given rate of interest, technical change that is Harrod-neutral will not alter the length of production processes. Other types of neutral technical progress, such as Hicks-neutrality, would alter the length of production processes for any given rate of interest.

In addition to this, some of the appeal of Harrod-neutrality as an assumption derives from the possibility that a growth model which displays this form of technical progress can conform to the stylized facts of growth in the long run. A model that does not display Harrod-neutrality cannot conform to the stylized facts of growth as they were discussed in chapter 1, where the ratio of factor shares, the capital-output ratio and the return to capital are constant over time, and the real wage, the capital-labor ratio, and the output-labor ratio are rising over time. Of course, if one or more of the variables which must remain constant over time for Harrod-neutrality to occur actually changes, then more than one type of technical progress might be consistent with the facts of economic growth.

Because the production parameters A_H and a_H are jointly determined, they will change each year in order to enable the model to track the actual data. The only production parameter which we will keep fixed is the elasticity of substitution s. This means that we will be seeing some non-neutral technical change as well as neutral change in our control run. However, we will vary only the rate of neutral (Hicks or Harrod) technical change.

In equation (3.1) we do not assume that "a" is constant from one year to the next. Because of this, we have the following (where M_K, M_L are the capital and labor shares):

$$\dot{A}/A = \dot{Q}/Q - M_K(\dot{K}/K) - M_L(\dot{L}/L) - [s/(s - 1)][A/Q]^{(s-1)/s}$$
$$\times [K^{(s-1)/s} - L^{(s-1)/2}](\dot{a}).$$

The last term is quite small, and although the rate of productivity change (neutral and non-neutral) is not exactly equal to $\dot{A}/A$, it is not far from it. In this paper, we set $\dot{A}/A$ equal to zero or vary it in other ways for our simulations, rather than changing $\dot{A}/A + [\dot{a}]$ (coefficient). Any changes in variables which we simulate are due to changes in the rate of Hicks-neutral productivity change.

In addition, it is not true in general that the assumption of a Harrod-neutral functional form for the production functions reduces the rate of change of the "a" (or a_H) parameter. For some of the sectors this is the case, but for others it is not. Thus a Harrod-neutral specification of the production function is not an obvious improvement over the specification which we choose to use.

2. It might be argued that the technology which a particular firm employs is a result of decisions to perform research and development, and also to imitate other firms. In addition, one might argue that a firm's search for new techniques depends on economic variables, including the firm's current profitability, and on technology spillovers from other industries. For examples of models which employ these kinds of assumptions, one can examine Nelson and Winter (1977a, 1977b) and Nelson, Winter and Schuette. In light of these theories, might changes in agricultural total factor productivity change have affected rates of productivity change in other industries?

Suppose that lower rates of growth of agricultural productivity had affected other industries' growth rates of productivity. For example, higher agricultural prices resulting from lower productivity growth might have induced greater productivity change in the industries using agricultural products. Then our assumption would overestimate the total effect of changes in agricultural total factor productivity change. On the other hand, if agricultural productivity growth is caused by progress in science which also affects other industries, then our assumption may be an underestimate of the total effect of agricultural productivity change. In the absence of a presumption that industry productivity changes are positively or negatively related to each other, we will maintain our hypothesis.

3. If $Y_t = \ln(X_t) - \ln(X_{t-1})$, then $X_t = \exp[Y_t]X_{t-1}$.

For a more complete explanation of the properties of Divisia indices, see Hulten (1973).

4. Simulations by Nelson and Winter (1977b) and Nelson, Winter and Schuette suffer from this problem. See chapter 2, p. 38.

5. For a discussion of the importance of this issue for policy, see Nelson and Winter (1976), p. 38.

6. When we speak of "aggregate capital," "overall capital," or just "capital," either prices or quantities, we mean a function of individual capital types, as in (3.2). The same holds for labor. When individual capital types are discussed, they will be named individually.

7. When we speak of "productivity growth," we mean the rise in A in (3.1) [e.g., $\dot{A}/A$ in (3.4)], or in other words total factor productivity growth. Labor productivity, when it is discussed, will be clearly differentiated.

8. If we believe that agricultural productivity change is, in fact, endogeneous, agricultural price changes might have been a causal factor inducing labor to leave the agricultural sector, and this in turn might affect technical change. Thus our results here might be occuring from a misspecification. However, to take into account the possible endogeneity of technology would require taking research and development into account, and we do not believe that the data in this area are good enough to enable meaningful results to be derived.

9. This is derived by taking the first order conditions for profit maximization and substituting them into the equation $PQ = wL + rK$. Output price here equals input price divided by the Hicksian parameter.

10. Denison (1974), pp. 43-44. Although we do not specifically account for education as a separate contribution toward labor input, to the extent that higher education leads to movement between occupations, it will be taken into account in our occupation measures. Also, labor characteristics were used in deriving the labor input data.

11. Ibid. p. 47.

12. Becker, Gary, *Human Capital* (1964), table 14, as reprinted in Welch (1970), p. 36.

13. Welch (1970), p. 35.

14. The amount of each labor input type is maintained unchanged in all runs. Nevertheless, the equations which determine aggregate labor as functions of individual labor types $[L_i = G_i(L_{1i}, L_{2i}, L_{3i})]$ do differ between sectors. Thus reallocation of labor inputs could conceivably cause overall labor input to decrease more than capital does, thereby causing K/L to fall. However, this is not what happens in this run.

15. It is not hard to construct simple examples where a declining aggregate K/L ratio is consistent with rising sectoral K/L ratios. Suppose the following situation occurs in a two-industry, two-period case (subscripts indicate industry):

    Period 1.

    Capital-labor ratios:
    $$K_1/L_1 = 62.5/41.67 = 1.5 \qquad K_2/L_2 = 17.5/58.33 = .3.$$
    Output shares:
    $$Sh_1 = \frac{K_1 + L_1}{\bar{K} + \bar{L}} = .5787 \qquad Sh_2 = \frac{K_2 + L_2}{\bar{K} + \bar{L}} = .4213.$$
    Endowment of K and L:
    $$K_1 + K_2 = \bar{K} = 80 \qquad L_1 + L_2 = \bar{L} = 100.$$

    Period 2.

    Capital-labor ratios:
    $$K_1/K_1 = 51.2/32.0 = 1.6 \qquad K_2/L_2 = 23.8/68.0 = .35.$$
    Output shares:
    $$Sh_1 = .4754 \qquad Sh_2 = .5246.$$
    Endowment of K and L:
    $$K_1 + K_2 = \bar{K} = 75 \qquad L_1 = L_2 = \bar{L} = 100.$$

    Percentage changes between Period 1 and Period 2:

    $$\% \; Chg \; [K_1/L_1] = 6.67\% \qquad \% \; Chg \; [K_2/L_2] = 16.67\%$$
    $$\% \; Chg \; [\bar{K}/\bar{L}] = -6.25\%.$$

16. The three exceptions are all for labor input: run 3—equipment, run 4—miscellaneous, and run 6—agriculture.

17. With one exception, the construction industry in run 6.

18. The only exceptions to these results are for run 10, where construction productivity change decreases and inputs do also. This is because demand for construction output decreases strongly in response to a rise in relative price, which is not true for agricultural output.

19. There are four industries producing consumption goods (agriculture, services, miscellaneous, and manufacturing) as opposed to the two that produce capital goods.

20. The ratio of personal consumption expenditure (PCE) to national income in this run rises when evaluated at old prices, but falls slightly when evaluated at new prices. Thus the ratio does not show a clear change.

Chapter 4

1. Hulten (1978), p. 511.

2. See Read (1968), Rymes (1971), and Hicks (1965).

3. Hulten (1975), p. 961.

4. Ibid. (1975), pp. 961-62.

5. Ibid. (1975), pp. 963-64.

6. This derivation closely follows Hulten (1975), pp. 958-60.

7. Ibid., pp. 959-60.

8. Ibid.

9. We present the sectoral effective rates of productivity change here. We could also compute Hulten's long-run Fisherian rate of technical change by sector. However, we do not do so. The long-run Fisherian rate by sector was derived for a model in which there was only one capital good and one capital goods sector. The presence of a second capital good and an investment process based on rates of return changes the meaning of the Fisherian rate. In this case, the Fisherian residual by sector is no longer meaningful.

10. Our terminology here is changed from Hulten's.

11. Hulten (1978), p. 514.

12. Hulten (1979), p. 130.

13. Ibid. (1979), p. 127.

14. The following discussion closely follows Hulten (1979). See also Malinvaud, E. "Capital Accumulation and Efficient Allocation of Resources." *Econometrica* **21** (1953), 233-69, and Malinvaud, E. "The Analogy Between Atemporal and Intertemporal Theories of Resource Allocation." *Review of Economic Studies* **28** (1961), 143-60.

15. Hulten (1979), p. 131, equation 19.

16. The 21.6% figure results from subtracting 49.06% (the total productivity change figure from tables 4.1, 4.4, and 4.5) from 70.69%.

Bibliography

Literature

Abramowitz, M. "Resource and Output Trends in the U.S. Since 1870." *American Economic Review* **46** (1956), 5-23.

Ahmad, S. "On the Theory of Induced Invention." *Economic Journal* **76** (1966), 344-57.

Aigner, D.J., and Chu, S.F. "On Estimating the Industry Production Function." *American Economic Review* **58** (1968), 826-39.

Allingham, M.G. "Tatonnement Stability: An Econometric Approach." *Econometrica* **40** (1972), 27-41.

Arnott, R.J., and Mackinnon, J.G. "The Effects of the Property Tax: A General Equilibrium Simulation." *Journal of Urban Economics* **4** (1977), 389-407.

Arrow, K.J. "Higher Education as a Filter." *Journal of Public Economics* **2** (1973), 193-216.

_____, Chenery, H., Minhas, B., and Solow, R. "Capital-Labor Substitution and Economic Efficiency." *Review of Economics and Statistics* **43** (1961), 225-50.

Atkinson, A.B. *The Economics of Inequality.* Oxford, Clarendon Press, 1974.

Bacharach, M. "Estimating Non-Negative Matrices From Marginal Data." *International Economic Review* **6** (1965), 294-310.

Ballentine, J.G. "A Simple and Efficient Method of Calculating the Impact of Finite Tax Changes in a Two-Sector Model." *Southern Economic Journal* **44** (1978), 629-34.

Barger, H. "Embodied versus Disembodied Improvements." *Review of Economics and Statistics* **58** (1976), 372-75.

Barzel, Y. "Productivity and the Price of Medical Services." *Journal of Political Economy* **77** (1969), 1014-27.

Batra, R. "Hicks- and Harrod-Neutral Technical Progress and the Relative Stability of a Two-Sector Growth Model with Fixed Coefficients." *Journal of Political Economy* **78** (1970), 84-96.

Baumol, W. "The Macroeconomics of Unbalanced Growth." *American Economic Review* **57** (1967), 520-35.

Beckmann, M.J., and Sato, R. "Aggregate Production Functions and Types of Technical Progress: A Statistical Analysis." *American Economic Review* **59** (1969), 88-101.

Behrman, J.R. "Sectoral Elasticities of Substitution Between Capital and Labor in a Developing Economy: Time-Series Analysis in the Case of Postwar Chile." *Econometrica* **40** (1972), 211-326.

Berglas, E. "Investment and Technological Change." *Journal of Political Economy* **73** (1965), 173-80.

Berndt, E.R. "Reconciling Alternative Estimates of the Elasticity of Substitution." *Review of Economics and Statistics* **58** (1976), 59-67.

_____, and Christensen, L.R. "The Translog Function and the Substitution of Equipment, Structures and Labor in U.S. Manufacturing, 1929-1968." *Journal of Econometrics* **1** (1973), 81-114 (1973a).

_____. "Testing For the Existence of a Consistent Aggregate Index of Labor Inputs." *American Economic Review* **64** (1974), 391-404.

_____. "The Internal Structure of Functional Relationships: Separability, Substitution, and Aggregation." *Review of Economic Studies* **40** (1973), 403-10 (1973b).

Berndt, E., and Wood, D.O. "Technology, Prices, and the Derived Demand for Energy." *Review of Economics and Statistics* **57** (1975), 259-68.

Bierwag, G.O., and Grove, M.A. "Indifference Curves in Asset Analysis." *Economic Journal* **76** (1966), 337-43.

Binswanger, H. "A Microeconomic Approach to Induced Innovation." *Economic Journal* **84** (1974), 940-58.

Blackorby, C., and Russell, R.R. "Functional Structure and the Allen Partial Elasticities of Substitution: An Application of Duality Theory." *Review of Economic Studies* **43** (1976), 285-92.

Borch, K. "A Note on Uncertainty and Indifference Curves." *Review of Economic Studies* **36** (1969), 1-4.

Bowles, S. "Aggregation of Labor Inputs on the Economics of Growth and Planning: Experiments with a Two-Level CES Function." *Journal of Political Economy* **78** (1970), 68-81.

Brown, M. *On the Theory and Measurement of Technological Change.* London, Cambridge University Press, 1966.

_____, and De Cani, J.S. "Technological Change and the Distribution of Income." *International Economic Review* **4** (1963), 289-309.

_____, and Heien, D. "The S-Branch Utility Tree: A Generalization of the Linear Expenditure System." *Econometrica* **40** (1972), 737-47.

Brubaker, E. "Multineutral Technical Progress: Compatibilities, Conditions, and Consistency with some Evidence." *American Economic Review* **62** (1972), 997-1003.

Burmeister, E., and Dobell, R. "Disembodied Technological Change with Several Factors." *Journal of Economic Theory* **1** (1969), 1-8.

_____. *Mathematical Theories of Economic Growth.* New York, MacMillan & Co., 1970.

Chenery, H., and Clark, P.G. *Interindustry Economics.* John Wiley and Sons, 1959.

Chipman J. "The Ordering of Portfolios in Terms of Mean and Variance." *Review of Economic Studies* **40** (1973), 167-90.

Christensen, L.R. "Entrepreneurial Income: How Does It Measure Up?" *American Economic Review* **61** (1971), 575-85.

_____, and Jorgensen, D.W. "The Measurement of U.S. Capital Input, 1929-1969." *Review of Income and Wealth* **15** (1969), 293-320.

_____. "U.S. Real Product and Real Factor Input, 1929-1967. *Review of Income and Wealth* **16** (1970), 19-50.

_____. "U.S. Income, Saving, and Wealth, 1929-1969." *Review of Income and Wealth* **19** (1973), 329-62.

_____, and Lau, L.J. "Conjugate Duality and the Transcendental Logarithmic Production Function." *Econometrica* **39** (1971), 255-56.

_____. "Transcendental Logarithmic Production Frontiers." *Review of Economics and Statistics* **55** (1973), 28-45.

_____. "Transcendental Logarithmic Utility Fuctions." *American Economic Review* **65** (1975), 367-83.

David, P., and Scadding, J.L. "Private Savings: Ultrarationality, Aggregation, and 'Denison's Law'." *Journal of Political Economy* **82** (1974), 225-49.

_____, and Van de Klundert, T. "Biased Efficiency Growth and Capital Labor Substitution in the U.S., 1899-1960." *American Economic Review* **55** (1965), 357-94.

Deaton, A. "A Reconsideration of the Empirical Implications of Additive Preferences." *Economic Journal* **84** (1974), 338-48.

_____, and Brown, A. "Models of Consumer Behavior: A Survey." *Economic Journal* **82** (1972), 1159-1236.

De Melo, J. "Protection and Resource Allocation in a Walrasian Model." *International Economic Review* 19 (1978), 25-43 (1978a).

———. "Estimating the Costs of Protection: A General Equilibrium Approach." *Quarterly Journal of Economics* 92 (1978), 209-26 (1978b).

Denison, E.F. *The Sources of Economic Growth in the U.S. and the Alternatives Before Us.* Committee for Economic Development, New York, 1962.

———. *Accounting for U.S. Economic Growth, 1929-1969.* The Brookings Institution, Washington, D.C., 1974.

———, assisted by Poullier, J.P. *Why Growth Rates Differ: Postwar Experience in Nine Western Countries.* The Brookings Institution, Washington, D.C., 1967.

———. "Income Types and the Size Distribution." *American Economic Review* 44 (1954), 254-69.

———. "A Note on Private Saving." *Review of Economics and Statistics* 40 (1958), 261-67.

———. "The Unimportance of the Embodied Question." *American Economic Review* 54 (1964), 90-93.

———. "The Contribution of Education to the Quality of Labor: A Comment." *American Economic Review* 59 (1969), 935-46.

———. "Some Major Issues in Productivity Analysis: An Examination of Estimates by Jorgenson and Griliches." *Survey of Current Business* 52 (1972), 37-64.

———. "Effects of Selected Changes in the Institutional and Human Environment upon Output Per Unit of Input." *Survey of Current Business* 58 (1978), 21-44.

———. "Explanations of Declining Productivity Growth." *Survey of Current Business* 59 (1979), 1-24.

Denny, M., and Fuss, M. "The Use of Approximation Analysis to Text for Separability and the Existence of Consistent Aggregates." *American Economic Review* 67 (1977), 404-18.

Diamond, P. "Technical Change and the Measurement of Capital and Output." *Review of Economic Studies* 32 (1965), 289-98 (1965a).

———. "Disembodied Technical Change in a Two-Sector Model." *Review of Economic Studies* 32 (1965), 161-68 (1965b).

———, McFadden, D., and Rodriguez, M. "Measurement of the Elasticity of Factor Substitution and Bias of Technical Change." Mimeo, to appear in *An Econometric Approach to Production Theory.*

Diewert, W.E. "Exact and Superlative Index Numbers." *Journal of Econometrics* 4 (1976), 115-45.

———. "An Application of the Shepard Duality Theorem: A Generalized Leontief Production Function." *Journal of Political Economy* 79 (1971), 481-507.

Domar, E.D. "On the Measurement of Technological Change." *Economic Journal* 71 (1961), 709-29.

———. "On Total Productivity and All That." *Journal of Political Economy* 70 (1962), 597-608.

———. "Total Productivity and the Quality of Capital." *Journal of Political Economy* 71 (1963), 586-88.

Dougherty, C.R.S. "Estimates of Labor Aggregation Functions." *Journal of Political Economy* 80 (1972), 1101-19.

Fair, R. *The Short-Run Demand for Workers and Hours.* North-Holland Publishing Company, Amsterdam, 1969.

Fallon, P.R., and Layard, P.R.G. "Capital-Skill Complementarity, Income Distribution, and Output Accounting." *Journal of Political Economy* 83 (1975), 279-301.

Feldstein, M. "Social Security, Induced Retirement, and Aggregate Capital Accumulation." *Journal of Political Economy* 82 (1974), 905-26.

———. "Mean-Variance Analysis in the Theory of Liquidity Preference and Portfolio Selection." *Review of Economic Studies* 36 (1969), 5-12.

Ferguson, C.E. "Cross-Section Production Functions and the Elasticity of Substitution in American Manufacturing Industry." *Review of Economics and Statistics* 45 (1963), 305-13.

Fishburn, P. "Mean-Risk Analysis with Risk Associated with Below-Target Returns." *American Economic Review* 67 (1977), 116-26.

Fisher, F.M. "The Existence of Aggregate Production Functions." *Econometrica* 37 (1969), 553-77 (1969a).

_____. "Approximate Aggregation and the Leontief Conditions." *Econometrica* 37 (1969), 457-69 (1969b).

_____. "Embodied Technical Change and the Existence of an Aggregate Capital Stock." *Review of Economic Studies* 32 (1965), 263-88.

_____. "Embodied Technology and the Aggregation of Fixed and Movable Capital Goods." *Review of Economic Studies* 35 (1968), 417-28.

Fraumeni, B.M., and Jorgenson, D.W. "The Sectoral Sources of Aggregate U.S. Economic Growth 1948-1976." Mimeo, 1979.

Gjeddebaek, N.F. "Contribution to the Study of Grouped Observations." *Skandinaviskaktuarietidskrift* 1949, 135-59.

Goldsmith, R. "A Perpetual Inventory of National Wealth." *Studies in Income and Wealth,* NBER, 14 (1951), 5-61.

Gollop, F. "Labor Input and the Decomposition of Labor Quality." Mimeo, 1977.

_____, and Jorgenson, D.W. "U.S. Productivity Growth by Industry, 1947-1973." Working paper, Social Systems Research Institute, 1977.

Gordon, R.J. "$45 Billion of U.S. Private Investment has been Mislaid." *American Economic Review* 59 (1969), 221-38.

_____. "$45 Billion of U.S. Private Investment has been Mislaid: Reply." *American Economic Review* 60 (1970), 940-45.

_____. "Measurement Bias in Price Indexes for Capital Goods." *Review of Income and Wealth* 17 (1971), 121-74.

Gorman, W.M. "Separable Utility and Aggregation." *Econometrica* 27 (1959), 469-81.

Grant, A. "Issues in Distribution Theory: The Measurement of Labor's Relative Share, 1899-1929." *Review of Economics and Statistics* 45 (1963), 273-79.

Green, H.A.J. "Embodied Progress, Investment, and Growth." *American Economic Review* 56 (1966), 138-51.

_____. *Aggregation in Economic Analysis: An Introductory Survey.* Princeton, Princeton University Press, 1964.

Greenwood, M.J. "An Analysis of the Determinants of Geographic Labor Mobility in the United States." *Review of Economics and Statistics* 51 (1969), 189-94.

Gregory, R.G., and James, D.W. "Do New Factories Embody Best Practice Technology." *Economic Journal* 83 (1973), 1133-55.

Griliches, Z. "The Sources of Measured Productivity Growth, U.S. Agriculture, 1940-1960." *Journal of Political Economy* 71 (1963), 331-46.

_____. "Research Expenditures, Education, and the Aggregate Agricultural Production Function." *American Economic Review* 54 (1964), 961-74.

_____. "Capital-Skill Complementarity." *Review of Economics and Statistics* 51 (1969), 465-68.

_____. "Issues in Assessing the Contribution of Research and Development to Productivity Growth." *Bell Journal of Economics* 5 (1979), 92-116.

_____, and Jorgenson, D. "Sources of Measured Productivity Change: Capital Input." *American Economic Review* 56 (1966), 50-61.

Hall, R.E. "Technical Change and Capital from the Point of View of the Dual." *Review of Economic Studies* 35 (1968), 35-46.

_____. "The Specification of Technology with Several Kinds of Output." *Journal of Political Economy* 81 (1973), 878-92.

_____, and Jorgenson, D.W. "Tax Policy and Investment Behavior." *American Economic Review* 57 (1967), 391-414.

Hanoch, G., and Levy, H. "The Efficiency Analysis of Choices Involving Risk." *Review of Economic Studies* 36 (1969), 335-46.

Harberger, A. "The Incidence of the Corporation Income Tax." *Journal of Political Economy* 70 (1962), 215-40.

Harris, R., and Mackinnon, J. "Computing Optimal Tax Equilibria." *Journal of Public Economics* **11** (1979), 197-212.

Hicks, J.R. *Capital and Growth.* Oxford University Press, London, 1965.

Hoffman, R.F. "Disaggregation and Calculations of the Welfare Cost of a Tax." *Journal of Political Economy* **80** (1972), 409-17.

Hudson, E.A., and Jorgenson, D.W. "U.S. Energy Policy and Economic Growth, 1975-2000." *Bell Journal of Economics and Management Science* **5** (1974), 461-514.

Hulten, C.R. "Divisia Index Numbers." *Econometrica* **41** (1973), 1017-23.

———. "Technical Change and the Reproducibility of Capital." *American Economic Review* **65** (1975), 956-65.

———. "Growth Accounting with Intermediate Inputs." *Review of Economic Studies* **45** (1978), 511-19.

———. "On the 'Importance' of Productivity Change." *American Economic Review* **69** (1979), 126-36.

———, and Nishimizu, M. "The Sources of Japanese Economic Growth." *Review of Economics and Statistics* **60** (1978), 351-61.

Humphrey, D.B., and Moroney, J.R. "Substitution among Capital, Labor, and National Resource Products in American Manufacturing." *Journal of Political Economy* **83** (1975), 57-82.

Intriligator, M.D. "Embodied Technical Change and Productivity in the United States, 1929-1958." *Review of Economics and Statistics* **47** (1965), 65-70.

Jaszi, G. "$45 Billion of U.S. Private Investment has been Mislaid: Comment." *American Economic Review* **60** (1970), 934-39.

Johansen, L.: "A Method for Separating the Effects of Capital Accumulation and Shifts in Production Functions Upon Growth in Labor Productivity." *Economic Journal* **71** (1961), 775-82.

Johnson, H.G., and Mieskowski, P.M. "The Effects of Unionization on the Distribution of Income: A General Equilibrium Approach." *Quarterly Journal of Economics* **84** (1970), 539-61.

Jorgenson, D.W. "The Embodiment Hypothesis." *Journal of Political Economy* **74** (1966), 1-17.

———. "The Economic Theory of Replacement and Depreciation." In *Essays in Honor of Jan Tinbergen,* edited by W. Sellekaerts, New York, 1973.

———, and Griliches, Z. "The Explanation of Productivity Change." *Review of Economic Studies* **34** (1967), 349-83.

———. "Issues in Growth Accounting: A Reply to Edward F. Denison." *Survey of Current Business* **52** (1972), 65-94.

———. "Final Reply." *Survey of Current Business* **52** (1972), 111.

———. "Divisia Index Numbers and Productivity Measurement." *Review of Income and Wealth* **17** (1971), 227-29.

Kendrick, J. *Productivity Trends in the United States.* Princeton, Princeton University Press, 1961.

———, assisted by Pech, M. *Postwar Productivity Trends in the U.S., 1948-1969.* New York, NBER, 1973.

———, with Lee, K.S., and Lomask, J. *The National Wealth of the United States: By Major Sectors and Industry.* New York, The Conference Board, 1976 (1976a).

———, assisted by Letham, Y. and Rowley, J. *The Formation and Stocks of Total Capital.* New York, NBER, 1976 (1976b).

———, and Sato, R. "Factor Prices, Productivity, and Economic Growth." *American Economic Review* **53** (1963), 974-1003.

Kennedy, C. "The Character of Improvements and of Technical Progress." *Economic Journal* **72** (1962), 899-911 (1962a).

———. "Harrod on 'Neutrality'." *Economic Journal* **72** (1962), 249-50 (1962b).

———, and Thirlwall, A.P. "Surveys in Applied Economics, and Technical Progress." *Economic Journal* **82** (1972), 11-72.

King, A.T. "Computing General Equilibrium Prices for Spatial Economies." *Review of Economics and Statistics* **59** (1977), 340-50.

———. "General Equilibrium with Externalities: A Computational Method and Urban Applications." *Journal of Urban Economics* **7** (1980), 84-101.

King, M.A. "Primary and Secondary Indicators of Education." In *Social Indicators and Social Policy,* edited by Shonfield, A., and Shaw, S., Social Science Research Council, 1972.

Kmenta, J. "On Estimation of the CES Production Function." *International Economic Review* **8** (1967), 180-89.

Koopmans, T.C., and Hansen, T. "On the Definition and Computation of a Capital Stock Invariant under Optimization." *Journal of Economic Theory* **5** (1972), 487-523.

Kravis, I.B. "Relative Income Shares in Fact and Theory." *American Economic Review* **49** (1959), 917-49.

Leigh, D. *An Analysis of the Determinants of Occupational Upgrading.* New York, Academic Press, 1978.

Levenson, I. "Reductions in Hours of Work as a Source of Productivity Growth." *Journal of Political Economy* **75** (1967), 199-204.

Levine, H.S. "A Small Problem in the Analysis of Growth." *Review of Economics and Statistics* **42** (1960), 225-28.

Lin, S.A.Y. "Generalized CES Production Functions." *Journal of Economic Theory* **3** (1971), 105-8.

Lintner, J. "The Valuation of Risk Assets and the Selection of Risky Investments in Stock Portfolios and Capital Budgets." *Review of Economics and Statistics* **47** (1965), 13-37.

Liviatan, N. "Multiperiod Future Consumption as an Aggregate." *American Economic Review* **56** (1966), 828-40.

———. "The Principle of Two-Stage Maximization in Price Theory." In *Value, Capital, and Growth: Essays in Honor of Sir John Hicks,* edited by J.N. Wolfe, Chicago, Aldine, pp. 291-303.

———. "A Diagrammatic Exposition of Optimal Growth." *American Economic Review* **60** (1970), 302-9.

Lovell, C.A.K. "A Note on Aggregation Bias and Loss." *Journal of Econometrics* **1** (1973), 301-11.

Lucas, R.E. "Labor-Capital Substitution in U.S. Manufacturing." In *The Taxation of Income from Capital,* edited by Harberger, A.C., and Bailey, M.J., The Brookings Institution, Washington, D.C., 1969.

McFadden, D. "Constant Elasticity of Substitution Production Functions." *Review of Economic Studies* **30** (1963), 73-83.

McKinnon, R.I. "Wages, Capital Costs, and Employment in Manufacturing: A Model Applied to 1947-1958 U.S. Data." *Econometrica* **30** (1962), 501-21.

McLure, C.E., Jr. "General Equilibrium Analysis: The Harberger Model After Ten Years." *Journal of Public Economics* **3** (1975), 125-61.

MacKinnon, J. "Solving General Equilibrium Models by the Sandwich Method." In *Fixed Points: Algorithms and Applications,* edited by Karamardian, S., and Garcia, C.B., New York, Academic Press, 1977.

Markowitz, H. *Portfolio Selection: Efficient Diversification of Investments.* New York, John Wiley and Sons, 1959.

———. "Portfolio Selection." *Journal of Finance* **7** (1952), 77-91.

Massell, B.F. "A Disaggregated View of Technical Change." *Journal of Political Economy* **69** (1961), 547-57.

———. "Another Small Problem in the Analysis of Growth." *Review of Economics and Statistics* **44** (1962), 330-32.

Mieskowski, P.M. "The Property Tax: An Excise Tax or A Profits Tax?" *Journal of Public Economics* **1** (1972), 73-96.

Miller, M.H., and Spencer, J.E. "The Static Economic Effects of the U.K. joining the EEC: A General Equilibrium Approach." *Review of Economic Studies* **43** (1977), 71-93.

Mundlak, Y. "Transcendental Multiproduct Production Functions." *International Economic Review* 5 (1964), 273-84.

Nadiri, M.I. "Some Approaches to the Theory of Measurement of Total Factor Productivity: A Survey." *Journal of Economic Literature* 8 (1970), 1137-77.

National Bureau of Economic Research. *The Behavior of Income Shares.* Studies in Income and Wealth, Vol. 27, Princeton University Press, Princeton, N.J., 1964.

Nelson, R.R. "Aggregate Production Functions and Medium-Range Growth Projections." *American Economic Review* 54 (1964), 575-606.

––––––. "The CES Production Function and Economic Growth Projections." *Review of Economics and Statistics* 47 (1965), 326-28.

––––––. "Recent Exercises in Growth Accounting: New Understanding or Dead End?" *American Economic Review* 63 (1973), 462-68.

––––––, and Winter, S.G. "In Search of Useful Theory of Innovation." *Research Policy* 6 (1977), 36-76 (1977a).

––––––. "Dynamic Competition and Technical Progress." In *Economic Progress, Private Values, and Public Policy: Essays in Honor of William Fellner,* B. Balassa and R.R. Nelson, eds., North-Holland, New York, 1977, pp. 57-101 (1977b).

––––––, and Schuette, H. "Technical Change in an Evolutionary Model." *Quarterly Journal of Economics* 90 (1976), 90-118.

Nishimizu, M. *Total Factor Productivity Analysis: A Disaggregated Study of the Postwar Japanese Economy with Explicit Consideration of Intermediate Inputs.* Unpublished Ph.D. dissertation, Johns Hopkins University, 1975.

Nordhaus, W.D. "The Recent Productivity Slowdown." *Brookings Papers on Economic Activity* 3 (1972), 493-536.

––––––. "Some Skeptical Thoughts on the Theory of Induced Innovation." *Quarterly Journal of Economics* 87 (1973), 208-9.

––––––. "The Falling Share of Profits." *Brookings Papers on Economic Activity* 5 (1974), 169-218.

Norsworthy, J.R., and Harper, M. "Productivity Growth in Manufacturing in the 1980's: Labor, Capital, and Energy." Paper presented at the American Statistical Association meetings, Washington, D.C., August 13, 1979 (1979a).

––––––. "The Role of Capital Formation in the Recent Productivity Slowdown." Bureau of Labor Statistics Working Paper No. 87, January 1979 (1979b).

––––––, and Kunze, K. "The Slowdown in Productivity Growth: Analysis of Some Contributing Factors." *Brookings Papers on Economic Activity* 9 (1979), 387-421.

Parks, R.W. "Systems of Demand Equations: An Empirical Comparison of Alternative Functional Forms." *Econometrica* 37 (1969), 629-50.

Pen, J. *Income Distribution: Facts, Theories, Policies.* Praeger Publishers, New York, 1971.

Perry, G. "Labor Force Structure, Potential Output, and Productivity." *Brookings Papers on Economic Activity,* 3 (1971), 540-65.

Pollak, R.A., and Wales, T.J. "Estimation of the Linear Expenditure System." *Econometrica* 37 (1969), 611-28.

Psacharopoulos, G., and Hinchliffe, K. "Further Evidence on the Elasticity of Substitution among Different Types of Educated Labor." *Journal of Political Economy* 78 (1972), 786-92.

Pratt, J.W. "Risk Aversion in the Small and in the Large." *Econometrica* 32 (1964), 122-36.

Read, L.M. "The Measurement of Total Factor Productivity Appropriate to Wage-Price Guidelines." *Canadian Journal of Economics* 1 (1968), 349-58.

Resek, R.W. "Neutrality of Technical Progress." *Review of Economics and Statistics* 45 (1963), 55-62.

Richter, M. "Cardinal Utility, Portfolio Selection, and Taxation." *Review of Economic Studies* 27 (1960), 152-66.

––––––. "Invariance Axioms and Economic Indexes." *Econometrica* 34 (1966), 739-55.

Rose, H. "The Condition for Factor-Augmenting Technical Change." *Economic Journal* **78** (1968), 966-71.

Rymes, T.K. "Professor Read and the Measurement of Total Factor Productivity." *Canadian Journal of Economics* **1** (1968), 359-67.

———. *On Concepts of Capital and Technical Change.* Cambridge, Cambridge University Press, 1971.

Salter, W. *Productivity and Technical Change.* London, Cambridge University Press, 1960.

Samuelson, P. "Two Generalizations of the Elasticity of Substitution." In *Value, Capital, and Growth: Essays in Honor of Sir John Hicks,* edited by J.N. Wolfe, Chicago, Aldine, 1968, pp. 467-80.

———. "A Theory of Induced Innovation Along Kennedy-Weizsacker Lines." *Review of Economics and Statistics* **47** (1965), 343-56.

———. "The Fundamental Approximation Theorem of Portfolio Analysis in Terms of Means, Variances, and Higher Moments." *Review of Economic Studies* **37** (1970), 537-42.

———. "General Proof that Diversification Pays." *Journal of Financial and Quantitative Analysis* **2** (1967), 1-13.

Sato, K. "A Two-Level Constant-Elasticity-of-Substitution Production Function." *Review of Economic Studies* **34** (1967), 210-18.

———. "On the Adjustment Time in Neo-Classical Growth Models." *Review of Economic Studies* **33** (1966), 263-68.

Sato, R. "The Estimation of Biased Technical Progress and the Production Function." *International Economic Review* **11** (1970), 179-203.

———. "Fiscal Policy in a Neo-Classical Growth Model: An Analysis of Time Required for Equilibrating Adjustment." *Review of Economic Studies* **30** (1963), 16-23.

———, and Beckmann, M. "Neutral Inventions and Production Functions." *Review of Economic Studies* **35** (1968), 57-66.

Scarf, H.E. "On the Computation of Equilibrium Prices." In *Ten Economic Studies in the Tradition of Irving Fisher,* New York, John Wiley and Sons, 1967.

———. "An Example of An Algorithm for Calculating General Equilibrium Prices." *American Economic Review* **59** (1969), 669-77.

———, in collaboration with Hansen, T. *The Computation of Economic Equilibria.* New Haven, Yale University Press, 1973.

Shoven, J.B. *General Equilibrium with Taxes: Existence, Computation, and a Capital Income Taxation Application.* Unpublished Ph.D. dissertation, Yale University, 1973.

———. "A Proof of the Existence of a General Equilibrium with ad valorem Commodity Taxes." *Journal of Economic Theory* **8** (1974), 7-25.

———. "Applying Fixed Point Algorithms to the Analysis of Tax Policies." In *Fixed Points: Algorithms and Applications,* edited by Karamardian, S. and Garcia, C.B., New York, Academic Press, 1977, pp. 403-34.

———. "The Incidence and Efficiency Effects of Taxes on Income from Capital." *Journal of Political Economy* **84** (1976), 1261-84.

———, and Whalley, J. "A General Equilibrium Calculation of the Effects of Differential Taxation of Income from Capital in the U.S." *Journal of Public Economics* **1** (1972), 281-321.

———. "General Equilibrium with Taxes: A Computational Procedure and an Existence Proof." *Review of Economic Studies* **40** (1973), 475-90.

———. "On the Computation of Competitive Equilibrium on International Markets with Tariffs." *Journal of International Economics* **4** (1974), 341-54.

———. "Equal Yield Tax Alternatives: General Equilibrium Computational Techniques." *Journal of Public Economics* **8** (1977), 211-24.

Simon, H. "Dynamic Programming under Uncertainty with a Quadratic Criterion Function." *Econometrica* **24** (1956), 74-81.

Solow, R.M. "A Skeptical Note on the Constancy of Relative Shares." *American Economic Review* **48** (1958), 618-31.

———. "Technical Change and the Aggregate Production Function." *Review of Economics and Statistics* **39** (1957), 312-20.

———. "Investment and Technical Progress." In *Mathematical Methods in the Social Sciences,* edited by Arrow, K.J., Karlin, S., and Suppes, P., 1959, pp. 89-104.

———. "The Production Function and the Theory of Capital." *Review of Economic Studies* **23** (1956), 101-8.

Star, S. "Accounting for the Growth of Output." *American Economic Review* **64** (1974), 123-35.

———, and Hall, R.E. "An Approximate Divisia Index of Total Factor Productivity." *Econometrica* **44** (1976), 257-63.

Steinberg, E. "Labor Mobility in 1960-65 and 1970-75." *Survey of Current Business* **59** (1979), 25-28.

Stiglitz, J. "A Two-Sector Two Class Model of Economic Growth." *Review of Economic Studies* **35** (1968), 227-38.

Stone, R. and Brown, J. *A Computable Model of Economic Growth: (A Programme of Growth 1).* London, Chapman & Hall, 1962.

Strotz, R.H. "The Empirical Implications of a Utility Tree." *Econometrica* **25** (1957), 269-80.

———. "The Utility Tree—a Correction and Further Appraisal." *Econometrica* **27** (1959), 482-88.

Tachibanaki, T. "Quality Change in Labor Input: Japanese Manufacturing." *Review of Economics and Statistics* **58** (1976), 293-99.

Takayama, A. "On Biased Technological Progress." *American Economic Review* **64** (1974), 631-39.

Taubman, P. *Sources of Inequality in Earnings; Personal Skills, Random Events, Preferences Towards Risk and other Occupational Characteristics.* Contributions to Economic Analysis, No. 96, New York, North Holland, 1975.

Terleckyj, N. "Estimates of the Direct and Indirect Effects of Industrial R&D on Economic Growth." In *Federal R&D Expenditures and the National Economy,* Hearings before the Subcommittee on Domestic and International Scientific Planning and Analysis, 94th Congress, 2nd Session, April 27, 28, 29, and May 4-5, 1976. No. 86.

Thurow, L.C., and Taylor, L.D. "The Interaction Between the Actual and the Potential Rates of Growth." *Review of Economics and Statistics* **48** (1966), 351-60.

Tobin, J. "Liquidity Preference as Behavior toward Risk." *Review of Economic Studies* **25** (1958), 65-86.

———. "Comment on Borch and Feldstein." *Review of Economic Studies* **36** (1969), 13-14.

Triplett, J. "Comment on the Impact on Econometric Models of the Present Treatment of Smog and Safety Devices in Economic Statistics." U.S. Department of Labor, Bureau of Labor Statistics, Working Paper 50, August 1975.

Tsiang, S.C. "The Rationale of the Mean-Standard Deviation Analysis, Skewness Preference, and the Demand for Money." *American Economic Review* **62** (1972), 354-71.

Uzawa, H. "Production Functions with Constant Elasticities of Substitution." *Review of Economic Studies* **28** (1960), 291-99.

———. "Neutral Inventions and the Stability of Growth Equilibrium." *Review of Economic Studies* **28** (1961), 117-24.

Wachtel, H.M., and Betsey, C. "Employment at Low Wages." *Review of Economics and Statistics* **54** (1972), 121-29.

Walters, A.A. "Production and Cost Functions: an Econometric Survey." *Econometrica* **31** (1963), 1-66.

Watanable, T. "A Note on Measuring Sectoral Input Productivity." *Review of Income and Wealth* **17** (1971), 335-40.

Welch, F. "Education in Production." *Journal of Political Economy* **78** (1970), 35-59.

Whalley, J. *A Numerical Assessment of the April 1973 Tax Changes in the U.K.* Unpublished Ph.D. dissertation, Yale University, 1973.

———. "A General Equilibrium Assessment of the 1973 U.K. Tax Reform." *Economica* **42** (1975), 139-61 (1975a).

_____. "How Reliable is Partial Equilibrium Analysis." *Review of Economics and Statistics* 57 (1975), 299-310, (1975b).

_____. "A Simulation Experiment into the Numerical Properties of General Equilibrium Models of Factor Market Distortions." *Review of Economics and Statistics* 59 (1977), 194-203 (1977a).

_____. "The United Kingdom Tax System 1968-1970: Some Fixed Point Indications of its Economic Impact." *Econometrica* 45 (1977), 1837-58 (1977b).

_____. "Fiscal Harmonization in the EEC; some Preliminary Findings of Fixed Point Calculations." In *Fixed Points: Algorithms and Applications,* edited by Karamardian, S., and Garcia, C.B., New York, Academic Press, 1977, pp. 435-72 (1977c).

_____. "General Equilibrium Analysis of U.S.-EEC-Japanese Trade and Trade Distorting Policies: a Model and Some Preliminary Findings." Working Paper, University of Western Ontario, London, Canada (1977d).

_____, and Piggott, J. "The Numerical Specification of Large-Scale Walrasian Policy Models." Working Paper, University of Western Ontario, London, Canada, 1977.

Wickens, M.R. "Estimation of the Vintage Cobb-Douglas Production Function for the United States, 1900-1960." *Review of Economics and Statistics* 52 (1970), 187-93.

You, J.K. "Embodied and Disembodied Technical Progress in the United States, 1929-1968." *Review of Economics and Statistics* 57 (1976), 123-27.

Zarembka, P. "On the Empirical Relevance of the CES Production Function." *Review of Economics and Statistics* 52 (1970), 47-53.

Zind, R.G. "A Note on the Measurement of Technical Bias in the U.S. Economy." *Review of Economics and Statistics* 61 (1979), 301-4.

Data

Bureau of the Census. "Subject Reports: Occupation and Residence in 1965." *1970 Census of Population* Pt. 7E, June 1973.

Bureau of Economic Analysis. "The Interindustry Structure of the United States: a Report on the 1958 Input-Output Study." *Survey of Current Business* 44 (1964), no. 11, 10-29.

_____. "The Transactions Table of the 1958 Input-Output Study and Revised Direct and Total Requirements Data." *Survey of Current Business* 45 (1965), no. 9, 33-46, 56.

_____. "Personal Consumption Expenditures in the 1958 Input-Output Study." *Survey of Current Business* 45 (1965), no. 10, 7-20, 28.

_____. "Input-Output Transactions: 1961." Staff Paper in Economics and Statistics, No. 16, 1968.

_____. "Input-Output Structure of the U.S. Economy: 1963." *Survey of Current Business* 49 (1969), no. 11, 16-47.

_____. "The Input-Output Structure of the United States Economy: 1947." March 1970.

_____. "Personal Consumption Expenditures in the 1963 Input-Output Study." *Survey of Current Business* 51 (1971), no. 1, 34-38.

_____. "Interindustry Transactions in New Structures and Equipment." *Survey of Current Business* 51 (1971), no. 8.

_____. "Input-Output Transactions: 1966." Staff Paper in Economics and Statistics, No. 19, February 1972.

_____. "The Composition of Value-Added in the 1963 Input-Output Study." *Survey of Current Business* 53 (1973), no. 4, 34-44.

_____. "The Input-Output Structure of the U.S. Economy: 1967." *Survey of Current Business* 54 (1974), no. 2, 24-56.

_____. "Interindustry Transactions in New Structures and Equipment, 1967." *Survey of Current Business* 55 (1975), no. 9, 9-21.

_____. *Interindustry Transactions in New Structures and Equipment, 1963 and 1967, I, II.* Washington, D.C., Government Printing Office, 1975.

_____. "Summary Input-Output Tables of the U.S. Economy: 1968, 1969, 1970." Staff Paper in Economics and Statistics, No. 27, September 1975.

_____. "Input-Output Table of the U.S. Economy: 1971." Staff Paper in Economics and Statistics, No. 28, March 1977.

_____. "Revised Input-Output Tables for the United States: 1967." Staff Paper in Economics and Statistics, No. 29, June 1977.

_____. *National Income and Product Accounts of the U.S., 1929-1974, Statistical Tables.* Government Printing Office, 1977.

Bureau of Labor Statistics. "Weekly and Hourly Earnings Data from the Current Population Survey." Special Labor Force Report No. 195, 1977.

_____. *Study of Consumer Expenditures, Incomes, and Savings. I. Family Accounts, 1950.* U. of Penn., 1956.

_____. *Consumer Expenditures and Income—Total United States, Urban and Rural, 1960-61.* BLS Report No. 237-93, February 1965.

_____. *Average Annual Expenditures for Commodity and Service Groups Classified by Nine Family Characteristics, 1972 and 1973.* BLS Report No. 455-3, December 1976.

Jack Faucett Associates, Inc. *Output and Employment for Input-Output Sectors: Time Series Data.* Jack Faucett Associates, Inc., No. 75-120. Prepared for the BLS, U.S. Dept. of Labor, March 1975.

_____. *Fixed Capital Stocks by Industry Sector, 1947-1974.* Jack Faucett Associates, Inc., No. 77-177. Prepared for the Bureau of Labor Statistics, U.S. Dept. of Labor, December 1977.

Index

Activity analysis. *See* Scarf algorithm
Additivity: of utility function, 9. *See also* Consumers, demand
Age, 45
Agriculture, 75; productivity change in, 49, 72-73, 93; and labor shares, 86, 87, 101
Approximation: to equilibrium, 7
Arnott, R.J., 8

Bacharach, M., 51
Becker, G., 74
Berndt, E., 15, 48
Bias: of productivity change, 109, 110
Biproportional matrix model. *See* RAS model
Break, G.F., 6
Business cycle: and model, 22, 97, 98-100; and units of input, 40, 41
Business transfers: as tax, 34; included in budget, 36-37

Capital consumption allowances, 10, 36. *See also* Saving
Capital gains: and capital income, 43; and investment, 27; and units of capital, 45
Capital-labor ratio, 62; in simulations, 62, 76-78, 89-90
Capital prices, 43, 113; in simulation runs, 70-72, 77, 84-86, 93
Capital shares, in simulations, 74-75, 87, 93
Capital stock, 2, 4; aggregation of, 13; as intermediate input, 114-15; endogeneity of, 2, 4, 5, 105; in simulations, 63-65, 78-80. *See also* Structures; Equipment
Christensen, L.R., 4, 15, 32, 34, 41, 48, 107
Cobb-Douglas. *See* Production function
Combinatorial topology, 7
Compensation, of labor, 48
Constant elasticity of substitution. *See* Production function
Constant returns to scale. *See* Linear homogeneity

Consumer prices, 14, 15, 26; in simulations, 68-69, 93
Consumers, 8, 11; demand and utility, 8-9
Consumption goods, 9, 26; and final demand, 50; by good and industry, 49, 54-55; prediction of, 100
Contributions for social insurance, 33
Control run: replicating economy's performance, 4
Convergence: of RAS model, 51, 52; of Scarf algorithm, 7
Corporate income tax, 34, 124 n.19

Data: consistency adjustments to, 31-32
David, P., 10, 11
Deaton, A., 9
Demand. *See* Consumers, demand
Denison, E.F., 74
Disembodiment. *See* Embodied Productivity change
Distortions: in economy, 8
Distribution of income: effects of productivity change on, 57; functional and relation to size distribution, 35
Divisia index: and average rate of productivity change, 59

Econometrics. *See* General equilibrium
Education, 45; increasing skills and income, 73-74
Elasticities: cross-price, 9; demand, 9, 10; income, 9, 10, 24; savings and interest, 10
Elasticity of substitution, 75; and productivity change, 103-4, 106-7; effects on factor shares, 87-89
Embodied productivity change, 5
Employment status: as labor characteristic, 45
Energy: 1975 crisis and prediction, 96. *See also* Prediction, Business cycle
Equilibrium: long-run, 6; short-run equilibrium assumed, 105

Equipment: as part of capital stock, 13,41; split from structures, 41-43. *See also* Structures
Estimation. *See* General equilibrium
Existence: of equilibrium, 7. *See also* Scarf algorithm
Expected utility, 29-30. *See also* Mean-variance
Exports: in final demand, 50

Factor augmentation, 23; and residual, 1, 123 n.2; different rates, of, 103
Factor prices: gross of tax, 14. *See also* Capital prices, Wages
Factor shares. *See* Capital share, Labor share, Incidence of productivity change
Feldstein, 125 n.20
Financial sector, 39
Fixed point. *See* Scarf algorithm
Functional distribution of income. *See* Distribution of income

General equilibrium: and econometric identification, 16; and noneconometric identification, 17; and parameter estimation, 16-17. *See also* Business cycle
Gollop, F., 46, 48
Government: budget and spending, 25, 37-39, 50; functions in Scarf algorithm, 7
Gross output: by industry, 35; growth of, 115-16; in simulation runs, 67-68, 81-84, 93

Harberger, A., 6, 8
Harrod-neutrality, 23, 128n.1
Hicks-neutrality, 23, 57; and Harrod-neutrality, 21; and production function, 62, 103-4; illustration, 3
Homogeneity: of consumer demands, 10; 125n.26
Hulten, C.R., 4, 107, 111

Identification. *See* General equilibrium
Imports: treatment of, in final demand, 51
Incidence of productivity change, expected results and algorithm, 4, 5, 6. *See also* Productivity change
Incidence of corporate income tax, 6. *See also* Distribution of income
Income tax, 10, 33
Indirect business taxes: as tax on output, 34
Inducted accumulation effect, 106, 109, 115
Industries, 12, 34; income by, 39; investment from, 54
Inferior goods: impossibility of, 9
Inflation, 6. *See also* Relative prices
Input: aggregate in simulations, 65-67, 78, 89; aggregate of capital and labor, 65, 105-6;

aggregate, prices in simulations, 70-72, 84-86, 96; effects of technical change on, 89
Input-output tables, 51, 52; and industry breakdown, 48; as data source, 32; matrix of coefficients, 14-15
Interindustry transactions. *See* Input-output. *See also* Intermediate input
Intermediate input: and productivity growth, 12; endogeneous, 105; in accounting framework, 114; in simulations, 67-68, 81-83, 93. *See also* Induced accumulation effect
Inventory change: as final demand, 41, 50
Investment, 53; and prediction, 100; and savings, 27, 28, 29; as final demand, 50. *See also* Mean-variance analysis

Jorgenson, D., 4, 32, 34, 41, 46, 107

King, A.T., 8
Kravis, I., 33

Labor, 2, 114; aggregation of, 13, 15; aggregation and occupational mobility, 47; benefits from productivity change, 72; characteristics of, 45; demand for, 14; in simulations, 65, 78-80, 89-90
Labor productivity. *See* Output-labor ratio
Labor shares: in simulations, 73, 87-88, 93
Land: treatment of, as capital, 41
Linear expenditure system. *See* Consumers, demand
Linear homogeneity: and consumption, 125 n.26; and long-run Fisherian rate, 108; and residual, 1
Loglinearity: of utility, 10

MacKinnon, J.G., 8
Macroeconomics, 6. *See also* Business cycle
Malinvaud, E., 4
Manufacturing: productivity change and factor shares, 87, 101
Marginal products: labor paid value of, 1, 18, 124 n.17
Mean return: on portfolio, 28
Mean-variance analysis: and capital goods demand, 27-30; and riskiness of assets, 45, 125 n.28. *See also* Von-Neumann, J.; Expected Utility.
Mieskowski, P., 34
Miller, M.H., 8
Model, 4; simulations, with, 4, 5
Morgenstern, O., 29-30
Monopoly, 18

National income and product accounts, 4, 17, 31, 36; and property tax in, 36

Nelson, R.R., 38, 127 n.19, 219 n.2

Occupations, 45-46; and mobility between, 46-47. *See also* Labor, Wages
Other labor income: as labor factor tax, 34
Output. *See* Gross output, Value-added
Output-labor ratio: and Hicks neutrality, 62; in simulations, 62-63, 78-79, 90

Parameters: for prediction, 96. *See also* General equilibrium
Perpetual inventory method: in defining capital stock, 113
Personal transfers to foreigners, 37. *See also* Government
Portfolio. *See* Mean-variance analysis
Prediction, 96-98
Price vector: in Scarf algorithm, 7
Producer prices, 14; in simulations, 68-69, 84-85, 93
Production functions, 11-12; alternatives to, 22; choice of parameters, 81-21; in Scarf algorithm, 7; non-neutrality of, 21
Productivity change: and effects on labor, 75; and factor intensity, 101; and factor shares, 73-75, 93, 100-101; and output and prices, 22, 84, 117; effective rate of, 104-5, 110-12, 116-17; effects on capital-labor ratio and capital, 76, 77-78, 104; exogeneity of, 124 n.11; long-run Fisherian rate, 108-10, 112; short-run Fisherian rate, 105-7, 112. *See also* Embodied productivity change, Residual
Productivity slowdown, 59, 61, 89
Profits: and productive techniques, 7
Profits tax. *See* Corporate income tax
Progressivity: of income tax, 10
Property taxes, 36, 43, 44; as tax on capital income, 34
Proprietors' income: as source of labor and capital income, 32-33

Race, 45
RAS model, 51-52, 54. *See also* Data
Research and development, 129 n.2
Residential structures, 41
Residual, 1, 103, 104, 112, 117; advantages of, 1; assumptions for, 1, 4; contribution to economic growth, 2, 3, 4; dynamic, 2, 3, 4, 5, 115; long-run Fisherian, 108-10, 111; short-run Fisherian, 105-7. *See also* Productivity change
Rotterdam model: non-additivity of, 10

Saving, 10; and capital consumption allowances, 36; and investment, 11, 27;

constant rate of 10, 11, 25, 125 n.20; corporate, 10, 35
Scadding, J.L., 10
Scarf algorithm, 6, 57; advantages of, 6, 7, 8; production in, 7. *See also* General equilibrium, Business cycle
Self-employment. *See* Employment status
Separability: of utility function, 9
Services, 90, 101
Sex, 45, 74
Shares. *See* Capital share, Labor share
Shoven, J., 6, 22
Simulations: list of, 58-61; performance of, 57-58; zero productivity growth run, 104-6
Size distribution of income. *See* Distribution of income
Social security. *See* Contributions for social insurance
Solow, R.M., 1, 2, 103
Solution: of algorithm, 7
Spencer, J.E., 8
Steinberg, E., 47
Structures: as part of capital stock, 13, 40; demand for, 13; split from equipment, 41-43. *See also* Equipment, Capital stock
Stylized facts of growth, 23-24; and Harrod-neutrality, 128 n.1
Subsidies less current surplus of government enterprises: as included in budget, 37

Taxes. *See* Contributions for social insurance, Corporate Income tax, Indirect business tax, Property tax
Translog production function. *See* Production function
Tsiang, 30

Unemployment, 6. *See also* Business cycle
Unionization, 8
Uniqueness: of equilibrium, 7. *See also* Scarf algorithm
Units, 33; of capital, 44-45; of labor, 48; of labor and capital, 18, 39-40
Utility: and risk aversion, 125 n.30; ordinal versus cardinal, 124 n.16
Utility tree: in consumption, 9

Value-added, 115; in simulations, 67-68, 81-84, 93
Variance: of return on portfolio, 28
Von Neumann, J., 29-30

Wages: and increased skills, 74; and labor shares, 74; differentials in, 16; in simulations, 70-72, 76, 77, 84-87, 93. *See also* Occupations
Walras' Law, 7, 25

Wealth: in accounting framework, 114;
ownership of, 10, 11, 35. *See also*
Consumers, demand
Whalley, J., 6, 8, 22, 35
Winter, S.G., 38, 127 n.19, 129 nn.2, 4